KAPLAN) pmbr

FINALS

CORPORATIONS

CORE CONCEPTS AND KEY QUESTIONS

Second Edition

T. Leigh Hearn, Esquire
Series Editor

This publication is designed to provide accurate and authoritative information in regard to the subject matter covered. It is sold with the understanding that the publisher is not engaged in rendering legal, accounting, or other professional service. If legal advice or other expert assistance is required, the services of a competent professional should be sought.

© 2009 by Kaplan, Inc.

Published by Kaplan Publishing, a division of Kaplan, Inc.
1 Liberty Plaza, 24th floor
New York, NY 10006

All rights reserved. The text of this publication, or any part thereof, may not be reproduced in any manner whatsoever without written permission from the publisher.

Printed in the United States of America

10   9   8   7   6   5   4   3   2   1

ISBN13: 978-1-60714-093-1

Kaplan Publishing books are available at special quantity discounts to use for sales promotions, employee premiums, or educational purposes. Please email our Special Sales Department to order or for more information at kaplanpublishing@kaplan.com, or write to Kaplan Publishing, 1 Liberty Plaza, 24th floor, New York, NY 10006.

TABLE OF CONTENTS

I. INTRODUCTION: THE CORPORATE FORM 1
   A. KEY CHARACTERISTICS OF CORPORATIONS 1
       1. Limited Liability
       2. Free Transferability of Shares
       3. Perpetual Existence
       4. Centralized Management
   B. PROBLEMS CREATED BY THE CORPORATE FORM 1
   C. CORPORATION STATUTES 1
   D. CORPORATIONS VERSUS OTHER BUSINESS ASSOCIATIONS 2
       1. General Partnership
           a. Liability
           b. Status as an association
           c. Transferability
           d. Equal management
           e. Authority
           f. Ownership
           g. Capacity for suits
           h. Taxation
           i. Termination
       2. Joint Venture
       3. Limited Partnership
       4. Limited Liability Partnerships
       5. Limited Liability Companies

II. FORMING THE CORPORATION 3
   A. PROPER FORMATION OF A CORPORATION 3
   B. EQUITY FINANCING 4
       1. Design of Securities
           a. Common stock
           b. Preferred stock
   C. LIMITED LIABILITY 4
           a. Benefits
               i. Decreasing the need to monitor
              ii. Reducing the costs of monitoring other shareholders
              iii. Promoting the free transfer of shares (and efficient management)
              iv. Facilitating the determination of fair share price
              v. Promoting efficient diversification (reducing the cost of raising capital)
           b. Background rule
   D. IMPERFECT CORPORATE FORMATIONS 5
       1. De Jure Corporations
       2. De Facto Corporations
       3. Corporation by Estoppel
   E. PIERCING THE CORPORATE VEIL 6
       1. Factors
           a. Alter ego
           b. Inadequate capitalization

CORPORATIONS

    c. Avoidance of contractual or statutory obligations
    d. Domination by a shareholder
    e. Commingling of assets
    e. Affiliated corporations
   2. Parent and Subsidiary Context
 F. **SUBORDINATION OF SHAREHOLDER CLAIMS**..................................7

III. PROMOTERS 7
 A. **DEFINITION**..7
 B. **FIDUCIARY OBLIGATION** 7
 C. **CONTRACTS ON BEHALF OF THE CORPORATION**..................................7
   1. Liability of Corporation
   2. Enforcement of Contract by the Corporation
   3. Liability of Promoters
   4. Enforcement of Contract by Promoter

IV. CAPITALIZING THE CORPORATION..8
 A. **PRE-INCORPORATION STOCK SUBSCRIPTION AGREEMENTS** 8
   1. Description
   2. Revocability of Pre-incorporation Subscription Agreements
    a. Majority rule
    b. Minority rule
   3. Rights of Subscribers
   4. Enforceability of Subscription Agreements
    a. Defenses
    b. Suits by subscribers
    c. Suits by the corporation
    d. Suits by corporate creditors where the corporation has become insolvent
 B. **REQUIREMENT OF ADEQUATE CONSIDERATION TO BE PAID FOR SHARES** 10
   1. Authorization and Original Issuance of Shares
   2. Issuance and Acquisition of Original Shares
    a. Description of "par" and "no par" value shares
     i. Par shares
     ii. "No par" value shares
    b. Consideration for shares
    c. Watered stock
   3. Recovery for Watered Stock
    a. By corporation (or its shareholders)
    b. By judgment creditors of the corporation
     i. Misrepresentation theory
     ii. Trust fund (or "statutory obligation") theory
    c. Original issuee liability
 C. **SPECIAL OBLIGATION OF PROMOTERS** 11

TABLE OF CONTENTS

V. MANAGEMENT OF THE CORPORATION'S AFFAIRS 12
   A. MANAGEMENT VESTED IN BOARD OF DIRECTORS 12
      1. Centralized Management
         a. Fundamental changes
         b. Ratification
         c. Close corporations or closely held corporations
      2. Benefits
   B. ULTRA VIRES DOCTRINE 12
   C. CONTROVERSIAL CORPORATE ACTIVITIES 13
      1. Long-term Contracts
      2. Political Contributions
      3. Charitable Donations
   D. ELECTION/APPOINTMENT OF DIRECTORS 13
      1. General Rule
      2. Cumulative Voting
         a. Description
         b. Example
      3. Qualifications
      4. Tenure of Office
      5. Resignation, Death, or Removal
         a. Removal without cause
         b. Removal for cause
         c. Removal under cumulative voting
         d. Removal by court action
      6. "De facto" Directors
   E. HOW THE BOARD OF DIRECTORS FUNCTIONS 15
      1. Notice of Board of Directors Meeting
      2. Quorum
      3. Informal Action
      4. Ratification
   F. DELEGATION OF AUTHORITY BY DIRECTORS 15
      1. Subcommittees
      2. Provisional Directors
      3. Nondirectors
      4. Voting Agreements
   G. CORPORATE OFFICERS AND AGENTS 16
      1. Appointment
      2. Removal
      3. Duties
         a. President
         b. Vice-president
         c. Secretary
         d. Treasurer
      4. Authority of Corporate Officers and Agents
         a. Actual authority
         b. Implied authority

CORPORATIONS

            i. Authority of office
           ii. By custom and practice
           iii. By apparent authority
       c. Ratification
   H. **COMPENSATION** 17
   I. **INSPECTION OF CORPORATE BOOKS AND RECORDS** 17

VI. **RESPONSIBILITIES AND DUTIES OF CORPORATE DIRECTORS AND OFFICERS** 17
   A. **DUTY OF CARE** 17
      1. Reasonable Inquiry
         a. Monitoring
      2. Business Judgment Rule
         a. Mere errors in business judgment are not actionable
            i. Policy arguments in favor of the business judgment rule
                (a) Institutional competence
                (b) Cost savings
                (c) Promotion of innovation and risk taking
                (d) Encourages well-qualified persons to serve
                (e) Other remedies are available
                (f) Protection of the shareholders
         b. Directors are not entitled to the presumption of the business judgment rule
      3. Defenses
         a. Nonparticipation or dissent
         b. Shareholder ratification
         c. Nondefenses
         d. Exculpation
      4. Oversight under Sarbanes-Oxley
         a. Corporate responsibility for financial reports
         b. Internal controls
         c. Whistleblower protection
         d. Audit committee
         e. Code of ethics
   B. **DUTY OF LOYALTY** 20
      1. Corporate Opportunity Doctrine
         a. Description of corporate opportunity
         b. Tests
            i. Line of business
            ii. Fairness
            iii. Interest or expectancy
            iv. Combination of line of business and fairness
            v. Interest or expectancy
         c. Remedies

2. Conflict of Interest Situations
    a. Valid quorum
    b. Interested director
    c. Interlocking directorships
    d. Entire fairness
    e. Remedy
3. Competition with One's Own Corporation

C. EXECUTIVE COMPENSATION..22
  1. Approval
  2. Past Services
  3. Fairness Review
  4. Future Services

D. REACQUISITION OF SHARES 23
E. ACQUISITION OF CORPORATE DEBT 23
F. DISTRIBUTION OF DIVIDENDS 23

VII. SHAREHOLDERS..23
A. VOTING..23
  1. Shareholder Meetings
      a. Notice
      b. Quorum requirements
  2. Voting
      a. Higher than "majority vote" requirements
      b. Voting by proxy
          i. Prohibited conduct
          ii. Definition
          iii. Disclosure
          iv. Solicitation
          v. Revocation
          vi. Shareholder proposals
              (a) Exceptions
          vii. Shareholder suits
      c. Pooling agreements
      d. Voting trusts
      e. Revocability and enforceability of pooling agreements and voting trusts
      f. Proxy contests
          i. Types
              (a) Control contest
              (b) Issue contest
          ii. Benefits of proxy contests
          iii. Reimbursement
              (a) Insiders
              (b) Insurgents
              (c) Is this unequal treatment good?

CORPORATIONS

    (d) What if reimbursement were contingent on success?
    (e) Reimbursement only for control contests
 B. PREEMPTIVE RIGHTS..28
  1. Common Law Rule
  2. Modern Rule
  3. Nonapplicability
  4. Equitable Considerations
  5. Remedies
 C. RIGHT TO RECEIVE DIVIDENDS..29
  1. Description of Dividends
  2. When Dividends May Be Paid
   a. Earned surplus
   b. Capital reduction surplus
   c. Paid-in surplus
   d. Revaluation (sometimes called "reappraisal") surplus
  3. Nimble Dividends
  4. Record Date
  5. Irrevocability of Dividends
  6. Consequences of an Improper Dividend
   a. Directors
   b. Shareholders
 D. DERIVATIVE ACTIONS 31
  1. Nature of Action
  2. Procedural Requisites
   a. Contemporaneous ownership of stock
   b. Demand upon directors
   c. Demand upon shareholders
   d. Security for expenses
   e. Independent committees
  3. Settlement or Dismissal
  4. Equitable Defenses
  5. Consequences of Litigation
  6. Indemnification of Directors or Officers
   a. Defendant successful on merits
   b. Pretrial settlement
 E. TRANSFERABILITY OF SHARES 34
  1. General Rule
  2. Reasonable Restrictions
  3. Unreasonable Restrictions
  4. Strict Interpretation
  5. Subsequent Limitations on Transferability
  6. Remedies
   a. Against the shareholder
   b. Against the transferee

TABLE OF CONTENTS

    F. **INSPECTION OF CORPORATE BOOKS AND RECORDS** 35
        1. Common Law Rule
            a. Burden of proof/common law
            b. Burden of proof/modern statutes
        2. Proper Purpose
        3. Improper Purpose
        4. Statutory Interpretation of Inspection Statutes
        5. Section 14(a) Rights

VIII. FIDUCIARY OBLIGATIONS OF MAJORITY OR CONTROLLING SHAREHOLDERS 36
    A. **GENERAL RULE** 36
    B. **EXAMPLES** 36
    C. **FREEZE-OUTS** 36
    D. **SHAREHOLDERS IN CLOSE CORPORATIONS** 36
    E. **SALE OF MAJORITY OR CONTROLLING INTEREST** 37
        1. General Rule
        2. Purchase of Directorships

IX. FUNDAMENTAL CORPORATE CHANGES 37
    A. **SALE OR TRANSFER OF ASSETS** 37
        1. Description
        2. Exceptions to Necessity for Shareholder Approval
        3. Appraisal Rights of Dissenting Shareholders
        4. Rights of the Corporation's Creditors
            a. Corporate liability
            b. Liability of the transferee
    B. **CORPORATE COMBINATIONS** 38
        1. Description
        2. Combination Types
            a. Merger and consolidation
                i. Statutory merger
                    (a) Necessary steps
                    (b) Short-form merger
                ii. De facto merger doctrine
                    (a) Description
                iii. Triangular merger
                iv. Compulsory share exchange
                v. Consolidation
            b. Exchange of shares (stock swap)
            c. Purchase of assets
        3. Appraisal Rights
            a. General rule
            b. Exceptions
            c. Effect of appraisal rights
        4. Rights of Creditors of the Target Corporation
        5. Acquisition or Purchase of Shares

CORPORATIONS

X. SECURITIES FRAUD AND INSIDER TRADING 42
    A. "SPECIAL FACTS" DOCTRINE 42
        1. Damages
        2. Corporate Action
        3. Direct Dealing
    B. SEC RULE 10B-5 42
        1. Unlawful
        2. Securities
        3. "Sale or Purchase Requirement"
        4. Instrumentality of Interstate Commerce
        5. "Purchasers or Sellers" Requirement
        6. Insiders
        7. Fraudulent or Manipulative Means
            a. Duty of disclosure
            b. False statements
            c. Negligent statements
        8. Materiality
        9. Reliance
       10. Civil Remedies
    C. SECTION 16(B) 43
        1. Securities Involved
        2. Director, Officer, or Ten Percent Shareholder
            a. Director
            b. Officer
            c. Ten percent shareholder
        3. Within Any Period of Less than Six Months
        4. Purchase and Sale, or Sale and Purchase, Requirement
        5. Corporate Recovery

XI. TENDER OFFERS AND TAKEOVER DEFENSES 45
    A. DEFINITION OF TENDER OFFER 45
        1. Shareholder Approval
        2. Board Approval
    B. FEDERAL REGULATION OF TENDER OFFERS 45
        1. No Secret Purchases
        2. Tender Offer Disclosure
        3. Timing
            a. Miminum offer period
            b. Withdrawal provision
            c. Policy considerations
        4. Equal Treatment
        5. Antifraud Provision
            a. Culpability
                i. Materiality
                ii. Reliance

TABLE OF CONTENTS

    iii. Remedies
     (a) Damages
     (b) Injunction
 C. STATE ANTITAKEOVER STATUTES 47
  1. First-Generation Statutes
  2. Second-Generation Statutes
   a. Control share acquisition statutes
   b. Fair-price statutes
   c. Redemption rights
   d. Moratorium statutes
 D. TAKEOVER DEFENSES 48
  1. Independence
  2. Pre/post-offer
   a. Pre-offer (prophylactic or "shark repellent") measures
   b. Post-offer measures
  3. Tactics Requiring/Not Requiring Shareholder Approval
  4. Definition of Selected Defensive Tactics
   a. Poison pill
    i. Variations
     (a) Rights plan
     (b) Conversion rights
     (c) Redemption rights
   b. Greenmail
    i. Impact on shareholders
    ii. Responses
   c. Restructuring defenses
    i. Leveraged buyout (LBO)
    ii. Recapitalization
    iii. Lockup
    iv. Self-tender
  5. The Case for Defensive Tactics
   a. Shareholders may make unwise decisions
    i. Distortions
     (a) Counterarguments:
    ii. The shareholders may be uninformed
    iii. Externalities
     (a) Counterarguments:
  6. The Case Against Defensive Tactics
   a. Policy arguments
    i. Acquisitions are good
     (a) Ex post
     (b) Ex ante
    ii. Therefore, obstructions are bad
     (a) Ex post
     (b) Ex ante

CORPORATIONS

        b. Legal arguments
            i. Potential conflict of interest
            ii. Corporate control market
            iii. Shareholder participation is viable

XII. DISSOLUTION AND LIQUIDATION 51
    A. DEFINITIONS..51
        1. How Do Corporations Dissolve?
        2. How Do Corporations Liquidate?

SAMPLE QUESTIONS 53
    MULTIPLE-CHOICE QUESTION TOPIC LIST 53
    MULTIPLE-CHOICE QUESTIONS 55
    ANSWERS TO MULTIPLE-CHOICE QUESTIONS 69

    TRUE-FALSE QUESTIONS TOPIC LIST 76
    TRUE-FALSE QUESTIONS 78

    ANSWERS TO TRUE-FALSE QUESTIONS 80
    ESSAY QUESTIONS..84
    ANSWERS TO ESSAY QUESTIONS 93

OUTLINE

I. INTRODUCTION: THE CORPORATE FORM

A. **KEY CHARACTERISTICS OF CORPORATIONS**: A corporation is a legal entity separate and distinct from its owners—the shareholders—having its own rights and obligations. Corporations are created under state law. Four characteristics have traditionally distinguished corporations from other forms of business organizations: limited liability, free transferability of shares, perpetual existence, and centralized management. Today the corporation shares these characteristics with other business forms such as the limited liability corporation (LLC).

1. **Limited liability:** The shareholder has only limited liability for corporation obligations; he or she is liable for them only to the extent of his or her investment.

2. **Free transferability of shares:** Shares, which represent ownership interests in a corporation, may be freely transferred. This characteristic creates liquidity where stock can be traded in active trading markets.

3. **Perpetual existence:** The corporation has an independent, perpetual existence, with no fixed date of dissolution.

4. **Centralized management:** There is centralized management in the corporation; decision-making powers are vested with the board of directors. Although shareholders are the owners, they do not make the decisions (except in limited instances).

B. **PROBLEMS CREATED BY THE CORPORATE FORM:** The key characteristics of the corporate form are not always advantages, and may create special problems for corporations. For example, limited liability raises the possibility of abuse of creditors, free transferability creates the possibility of insider trading, and centralized management creates the possibility of abuse of power. Each of these characteristics, then, may engender breaches of fiduciary duty.

C. **CORPORATION STATUTES:** Corporation statutes are state statutes that authorize the creation of corporations, describe their basic attributes, and provide standardized terms governing the relationship among shareholders, managers, and creditors that apply unless different firm-specific terms are chosen.

1. **The benefits of corporate statutes are:** (1) they reduce the transaction costs of corporate formation; and (2) they promote liquidity by allowing investors who wish to invest in a corporation to acquire shares without a close examination of the corporation's basic documents.

2. One detriment of corporate statutes is that, because companies choose the state of incorporation, competition among states flourishes—the so-called "race to the bottom." States attract corporations by creating pro-management rules.

CORPORATIONS

3. A majority of states have enacted corporation statutes based on the Model Business Corporation Act (MBCA), but several states, including Delaware, California, and New York most prominently, have enacted their own statutes. Delaware's corporation statue has been particularly significant, given that most large, publicly held corporations are incorporated in Delaware.

D. CORPORATIONS VERSUS OTHER BUSINESS ASSOCIATIONS

1. **General Partnership:** All states have adopted some version of the Uniform Partnership Act ("UPA"), which governs partnerships, or the more recent Revised Uniform Partnership Act ("RUPA"). RUPA has conferred onto partnerships entity status, and many more states will probably choose to adopt RUPA for this reason.

    a. **Liability:** Each partner is jointly and severally liable for partnership debts.

    b. **Status as an association:** A partnership is an association of two or more persons engaged in a business for profit as co-owners.

    c. **Transferability:** A partner may assign his interest in the partnership. The assignee receives distributions of the profit, but he does not become a partner. He can not, therefore, participate in the management of the partnership's affairs or exercise other rights of partners.

    d. **Equal Management:** Unless the partners explicitly decide otherwise, each partner in a partnership has an equal interest and plays an equal role in managing the partnership.

    e. **Authority:** Each partner acts as an agent of the firm. Therefore, each partner has the authority to bind the partnership in contractual and transactional situations, as long as such activities occur in the regular course of business.

    f. **Ownership:** While title may be held in the name of the partnership, partnership property is owned by the partners as tenants in the partnership. Under RUPA, no such tenancy exists, and all property is owned by the partnership entity.

    g. **Capacity for suits:** Under the UPA, a plaintiff must file suit against individual partners, not against the partnership. All partners are jointly liable for the debts and liabilities of the partnership and are jointly and severally liable for wrongful acts and breaches of trust.

    h. **Taxation:** Income of a partnership flows through the entity to the partners, who must pay taxes on that income. By contrast, corporate earnings are taxed at the entity level. If the corporation uses earnings to pay dividends to its shareholders, those dividends are taxable income for shareholders. Thus, when dividends are paid, corporate earnings are subject to double taxation.

    i. **Termination:** A partnership is terminable at will unless a fixed date of dissolution is expressed or implied unless otherwise provided in the partnership agreement. If a partner dies, becomes incapacitated, or withdraws, the partnership is automatically dissolved.

2. **Joint Venture:** A joint venture is basically a partnership formed for a single, limited business purpose, such as, for example, between two pharmaceutical companies collaborating on the development of a new drug.

3. **Limited Partnership:** A limited partnership has two classes of partners, general partners and limited partners. General partners have the same rights and obligations as do partners in a regular partnership. Limited partners, however, have no control over the management of the partnership but enjoy limited liability to the extent of their investment.

4. **Limited Liability Partnerships:** In a limited liability partnership ("LLP"), partners are liable for the partnership's contractual obligations, but if a partner is not personally involved in negligence, wrongful acts, or misconduct, the partnership, not he, is liable for any damages arising from such conduct.

5. **Limited Liability Companies:** A limited liability company ("LLC") is not a corporation, but rather a business entity whose members (the owners) may participate in managing the entity's affairs while retaining limited liability. Furthermore, nonmembers may participate in the management of the entity. LLC's may exist indefinitely or for a stated term. Various statutes provide for distributions in an LLC to be made either equally to each member or in proportion to each member's contribution.

    a. With an LLC, the entity itself is not taxed. Income of an LLC flows through distributions to its members, who report the income on their personal tax returns. Ownership interests may generally be structured as the members desire, and there is no limit on the number or type of owners. Both managers and owners enjoy limited liability. For all of these reasons, an LLC can be a very advantageous organizational form for nonpublicly held businesses.

II. FORMING THE CORPORATION

A. **PROPER FORMATION OF A CORPORATION:** If a corporation is not adequately formed, the existing entity is probably a partnership (in which event each partner is personally liable for the entity's obligations). Where a corporation is adequately formed, the shareholders have *no personal liability* for that entity's obligations. Their losses are limited to the consideration paid for their shares.

A corporation is ordinarily created by delivering a properly completed set of the Articles of Incorporation to the secretary of state, with any requisite filing fee.

1. The Articles of Incorporation are the corporation's "constitution." The articles are usually a simple document. They allow for flexibility, but can be difficult

CORPORATIONS

to amend, given that any amendment requires approval by the corporation's shareholders to take effect.

2. State statutes also generally require that following incorporation, a first organizational meeting be held so that the directors may be elected and the by-laws adopted.

B. **EQUITY FINANCING:** The corporation can issue shares of stock representing ownership interests in the corporation. As owners, shareholders have financial rights to dividends when and as declared by the board of directors, but possess only a residual claim on the assets of the corporation. Shareholders get paid only after all the other creditors have been paid. To protect their interests, shareholders have voting rights to elect directors and approve major corporate transactions (e.g., mergers, increases in shares of stock authorized for issuance).

1. **Design of securities:** A corporation's Articles of Incorporation will set forth the classes of equity securities the corporation is authorized to issue, and the number of shares, as well as the rights, preferences, privileges, and limitations, of each class of securities authorized for issuance.

    a. **Common stock:** Common stock carries with it ownership rights, but no fixed obligations. Holders of common stock possess only a *residual claim*; they get paid only after all other creditors have been paid. While common stock carries the highest risk, it also enjoys the greatest possibility of gain if the business is successful.

    b. **Preferred stock:** All securities other than common stock are referred to as "senior" securities. Preferred stock is the least senior of senior securities. Although it is a permanent investment in the corporation, preferred stock can be "redeemable," that is, purchased by the corporation at a defined price. Since common law presumes that stock is stock, preferred stock is entitled to the same voting rights as common stock, unless the Articles of Incorporation state otherwise, as they normally do.

C. **LIMITED LIABILITY**

1. One of the strongest reasons for attaining corporate status is limited liability for shareholders.

    a. **Benefits:** According to some experts, the formation of publicly held corporations facilitates the division of labor between those with managerial skills and those with capital (the risk-bearers). Limited liability reduces the costs associated with this division (the *agency costs*) by:

        i. **Decreasing the need to monitor:** Limited liability makes diversification and passivity more rational strategies than the close monitoring of the agents managing the enterprise, thereby reducing the costs of operating the corporation.

ii. **Reducing the costs of monitoring other shareholders:** Without limited liability, the greater the shareholder's wealth, the greater his potential liability. Shareholders would have an incentive to find out which shareholders have deep pockets. Limited liability makes shareholder identity irrelevant.

iii. **Promoting the free transfer of shares (and efficient management):** Limited liability reduces the cost of purchasing shares, which is determined simply by the present value of future cash flow. Shares are fungible, and, without limited liability, the share price becomes a function of the present value of future cash flow and the shareholders' wealth. The free transfer of shares facilitates the transfer of control, which in turn induces managers to operate efficiently to avoid such transfers of control (and to avoid being displaced).

iv. **Facilitating the determination of fair share price:** Where stock is publicly traded, the fungibility of shares enables investors to trade in the market in the same terms, and share prices come to reflect all available information.

v. **Promoting efficient diversification (reducing the cost of raising capital):** With limited liability, diversification lowers risk. With unlimited liability, however, diversification *increases* risk, since if any one firm goes bankrupt, the investor could lose it all. Therefore, with unlimited liability, the rational strategy is for the shareholder to minimize the number of securities held. The risk to the shareholder, however, is still higher than it would be with a rule of limited liability, and therefore the shareholder must expect a higher return, thereby increasing the cost of raising capital.

b. **Background rule:** Limited liability is the background rule, but parties can contract around limited liability. For example, shareholders can give personal guarantees for corporate debt.

D. **IMPERFECT CORPORATE FORMATIONS**

1. **De jure corporations:** Where there has been *substantial* compliance with the statutory requisites for formation, a de jure corporation exists (i.e., one that is sufficiently formed to be recognized as a corporation *for all purposes*). Ordinarily, Articles of Incorporation must have been filed to argue for the existence of de jure corporation, but some jurisdictions hold that a de jure corporation is formed where there has been compliance with all mandatory (as opposed to "permissive" or "directory") requirements.

2. **De facto corporations:** A "de facto" corporation exists where:

   a. There has been a "colorable" or "good faith" attempt to comply with the statutory requisites for formation, *and*

   b. There has been some actual use of the purported corporate existence, such as carrying on business publicly as a corporation.

CORPORATIONS

Although a de facto corporation may protect shareholders from personal liability for corporate obligations, the state may still challenge its existence by means of a quo warranto proceeding in which the ability of the entity to engage in business as a corporation is determined.

3. **Corporation by estoppel:** Where a person believed that he was dealing with a corporation, then *for purposes of that transaction,* neither side can deny (i.e., each party is estopped from denying) the existence of the purported corporate entity.

   a. This doctrine is premised on the unfairness of permitting a creditor, for example, to deny the existence of a corporation when he had dealt with the entity on that basis.

   b. The doctrine also works in reverse; a defendant that has held itself out to be a corporation cannot try to avoid liability by claiming that the plaintiff has no cause of action because the defendant is not a legal entity.

   c. This doctrine is ordinarily applicable to contractual or transactional types of situations only.

   De facto, and only against prise under agency or partnership theories of liability.

E. **PIERCING THE CORPORATE VEIL: Despite adequate formation of a corporation, the corporate veil may be "pierced" (i.e., the individual shareholders may be held personally liable for corporate obligations) when necessary "to prevent fraud or injustice."**

   1. **Factors**: Fraud or injustice has been found in the following circumstances to warrant piercing the corporate veil and holding shareholders personally liable:

      a. **Alter ego:** Where the shareholders fail to observe corporate formalities and to deal with the corporation as a separate, distinct entity (e.g., neglect to hold director and shareholder meetings, commingle corporate and private monies, etc.).

      b. **Inadequate capitalization:** Where the corporation was capitalized with assets that were inadequate to meet the obligations that a business of that nature could reasonably be expected to incur.

      c. **Avoidance of contractual or statutory obligations:** Where a corporation is formed by shareholders for the purpose of evading a contractual obligation (e.g., a noncompetition clause) or statutory laws (e.g., certain types of corporations cannot exceed a designated rate of interest).

      d. **Domination by a shareholder:** When one individual or corporation owns most or all of the stock and thereby controls policy and/or business decisions.

e. **Commingling of assets:** Where shareholders have siphoned off corporate funds or used corporate assets as if they were their own, or have commingled their personal assets with corporate assets.

f. **Affiliated corporations:** Where corporations have interlocking shareholders and perform different aspects of a single business operation or enterprise, courts have sometimes held that each corporation is liable for the others' debts.

2. **Parent and subsidiary context:** A corporation will often form subsidiaries to isolate business assets and risks. Typically, under these circumstances, a parent corporation is entitled to the benefits of limited liability, so that its exposure for liabilities of a subsidiary will be limited to the amount of the parent's investment in the subsidiary. However, if it can be shown that the parent so dominates the subsidiary that the two can be taken to act as a single entity, and treating the parent and subsidiary as separate entities would lead to injustice, a court will pierce the parent's corporate veil to hold it liable for claims made against the subsidiary. Studies have shown, however, that courts are less willing to pierce the corporate veil to reach a corporate defendant than an individual one.

F. **SUBORDINATION OF SHAREHOLDER CLAIMS:** In bankruptcy proceedings, shareholder loans are not automatically subordinate to outsider claims. Where a corporation's shareholders are, in some manner (i.e., via negligence or inattentiveness), responsible for their corporation's inability to pay its debts, obligations owed by the corporation to those shareholders may be equitably subordinated to the claims of the corporation's other creditors (the so-called "Deep Rock" doctrine, after the name of subsidiary whose parent corporation's claims on the subsidiary were subordinated to those of the subsidiary's preferred shareholders because the parent's claims arose from transactions entered into with the subsidiary on terms highly disadvantageous, and in violation of fiduciary duty, to the subsidiary).

III. PROMOTERS

A. **DEFINITION:** A promoter is a person who, prior to formation, prepares the corporation for commencing business and supervises compliance with the requisites necessary for it to come into existence. Unlike incorporators, promoters bear significant responsibility, particularly to creditors, for transactions entered into on behalf of the corporation prior to formation.

B. **FIDUCIARY OBLIGATION:** Prior to formation, promoters are, in effect, partners. They therefore owe a fiduciary obligation of full disclosure to the corporation and may not engage in self-dealing to the detriment of the corporation.

C. **CONTRACTS ON BEHALF OF THE CORPORATION**

1. **Liability of corporation:** A corporation is not liable for contracts made on its behalf by promoters prior to incorporation, unless the contract is expressly or

impliedly ratified by it after it has been formed. Absent a claim of unjust enrichment by a third party, the refusal of those in charge of the corporation to adopt the contract prevents liability for the company.

   a. Express ratification occurs where the contract is explicitly approved or adopted by the board of directors.

   b. Implied ratification occurs where the corporation accepts or acknowledges the benefits of the contracts in some manner. (A corporation may be liable under quasi-contract principles where it derives a benefit from a contract which it ultimately rejects or refuses to ratify.)

2. **Enforcement of contract by the corporation:** Upon ratification, a corporation may enforce the contract directly against the obligor.

3. **Liability of promoters:** Whether a promoter is personally liable under a contract he has entered into on behalf of a corporation when the corporation, after formation, fails to ratify or perform the agreement depends upon the intentions of the obligee and the promoter. Absent a contrary intent, the promoter is typically held personally liable on pre-incorporation contracts he enters into on behalf of a corporation.

   a. However, where the promoter specifically disclaims *personal liability,* the obligee will not be able to successfully maintain an action against him.

   b. But where the circumstances are ambiguous and the obligee was aware that no corporation had been formed, courts tend to hold that the obligee intended the promoter to be personally liable if the contract is not ratified (by the corporation and especially if the obligee incurred any detriment by reason of the agreement). The promoter may, however, be permitted to recover in quasi contract from the corporation to the extent that the latter entity benefits from the agreement.

4. **Enforcement of contract by promoter:** Upon ratification by the corporation, a promoter ceases to have any rights under the contract and may not enforce it. If, however, the corporation fails or refuses to ratify the contract, the promoter is usually permitted to enforce the agreement against the obligor.

IV. CAPITALIZING THE CORPORATION

A. PRE-INCORPORATION STOCK SUBSCRIPTION AGREEMENTS

1. **Description:** Pre-incorporation stock subscription agreements are "contracts" entered into between persons who promise to purchase a prescribed number of shares for a specified amount (the subscribers) from the corporation after it has been formed. Typically, a promoter signs on behalf of the corporation.

2. **Revocability of pre-incorporation subscription agreements**

    a. **Majority rule:** Subscription agreements are ordinarily viewed as a continuing offer to the corporation (i.e., since the corporation has not yet been established, there is no officer to validly execute the contract on its behalf). Unless there is legislation that precludes revocation for a prescribed period of time, a subscription agreement is revocable by a subscriber until the corporation has been formed and has accepted the offer. Several states have laws prohibiting revocation for a prescribed period of time.

    b. **Minority rule:** Some states take the view that a pre-incorporation subscription agreement is a contract among the subscribers, and the corporation, after it has been formed, is a third-party beneficiary. Under this view, a subscription agreement cannot be revoked unless all of the potential shareholders agree to release each other. These states ordinarily permit the corporation, after it has been formed, to enforce the contract.

3. **Rights of subscribers:** Unless the stock subscription agreement is viewed as an installment purchase contract (i.e., title to the stock remains in the corporation until the entire purchase price has been paid), a subscriber attains shareholder status as soon as the subscription contract has been accepted by the corporation (even if the subscriber is not required to pay the entire subscription price when the stock is initially tendered to him).

4. **Enforceability of subscription agreements**

    a. **Defenses:** A subscriber who is attempting to avoid his obligations under a subscription contract can assert any applicable contractual defense (e.g., fraud which is attributable to the corporation, lack of definiteness, etc.).

    Where the corporation becomes insolvent prior to the time a payment is due and owing, many jurisdictions do not permit the subscriber to assert material breach (i.e., the corporation's insolvency) as a defense to an action ***by creditors*** (the creditors are deemed to have implicitly relied upon the subscription agreement in extending credit to the corporation). A few states, however, permit this defense where the subscription agreement is viewed as an installment purchase contract.

    b. **Suits by subscribers:** A subscriber who fails to purchase the shares he promised to buy is liable to the other subscribers for any liability they incur as a consequence of the former's breach.

    c. **Suits by the corporation:** The breaching subscriber is liable to the corporation for the unpaid subscription price.

    d. **Suits by corporate creditors where the corporation has become insolvent:** Where a corporation has become insolvent, its creditors (or those

CORPORATIONS

acting on behalf of the creditors, such as a trustee-in-bankruptcy or receiver) can enforce subscription agreements. The breaching subscriber is liable for the corporation's obligations to the extent of their unpaid subscription obligations.

B. **REQUIREMENT OF ADEQUATE CONSIDERATION TO BE PAID FOR SHARES**

1. **Authorization and original issuance of shares:** Stock *originally* issued by a corporation must have been authorized by the Articles of Incorporation or by-laws of the corporation by the board of directors. Shares subsequently repurchased by the corporation may either be cancelled (in which case they cannot be reissued) or held as treasury stock (in which case they may be resold by the corporation).

2. **Issuance and acquisition of original shares**

    a. **Description of "par" and "no par" value shares**

        i. **Par shares:** Shares whose par value—the amount that must be paid for the shares for them to be considered "fully paid and nonassessable"—is stated in the Articles of Incorporation or by-laws.

        ii. **"No par" value shares:** Shares whose stated value is determined by the board of directors, based upon the corporation's status and assets at the time the shares are to be sold. As long as this determination is made in "good faith," it will rarely be subject to successful attack.

    b. **Consideration for shares:** Ordinarily, par and no par shares may be issued only for *full value.* "Full value" means money paid, labor actually done, or property transferred to the corporation, which is equivalent to the par or determined value (in the case of no par stock) of the share. Additionally, many jurisdictions permit acceptance of *adequately secured* promissory notes to constitute "full" payment.

        i. Where a corporation is in immediate need of capital, the board of directors is ordinarily permitted (i) to sell par value shares below the stated amount, and (ii) no par shares for an amount below their fair market value.

        ii. Many jurisdictions permit shares to be issued to directors, officers, or employees in payment for services *to be rendered* in the future. Under these circumstances, however, the shares are not "fully paid" until the services have actually been rendered.

    c. **Watered stock:** Stock is "watered" when it is issued for consideration which is less than its par value, or, in the case of no par stock, its agreed upon fair market value, but has nevertheless been designated as "fully paid." Where, however, labor is performed for, or property is transferred to, the corporation in exchange for shares, the "good faith" judgment of the directors as to the value of such property or services is rarely the subject of successful attack.

3. **Recovery for watered stock**

   a. **By corporation (or its shareholders):** In most jurisdictions, the corporation *cannot* recover the "watered" amount. It is estopped by having marked the shares as "fully paid" on its books. However, recovery is possible where the issuee obtained the shares by fraud or breaching a fiduciary duty. Individual shareholders *cannot* recover the watered amount, since an action for this type of loss lies with the corporation.

   There is an emerging view, however, that (1) the corporation may rescind the transaction (provided it acts within a reasonable period of time of issuance of the shares), or (2) recover the "watered" amount (i.e., the difference between the par or agreed upon value of the shares and the consideration actually received by the corporation).

   b. **By judgment creditors of the corporation:** There are two main theories pursuant to which creditors who have obtained a judgment against the corporation (or where the corporate entity has become insolvent, a trustee-in-bankruptcy or receiver) can recover the watered amount of stock.

      i. **Misrepresentation theory:** Under this theory, creditors who relied upon the stated capital of the corporation may recover an unpaid outstanding judgment from the original issuee of watered stock. While most states require the creditor's *actual* reliance upon the corporation's stated capital (i.e., such as that set forth in a financial statement), a few jurisdictions presume that credit provided to a corporation was made on the basis that its stock was "unwatered." Thus, only persons who became judgment creditors *subsequent* to the time that the watered stock was issued may recover under this theory.

      ii. **Trust fund (or "statutory obligation") theory:** Under this theory, the watered amount can be recovered from the original issuee by any creditor (regardless of when the obligation arose or whether there was reliance upon a stated amount of capital).

   c. **Original issuee liability:** Ordinarily, only the original issuee of watered stock is liable for the watered amount. A subsequent transferee of the watered stock has no liability, unless he was aware that the shares were issued for less value than the stated or agreed upon value.

C. **SPECIAL OBLIGATION OF PROMOTERS: Where a promoter is to receive stock in exchange for assets transferred, or services rendered to the corporation, he must ordinarily make full disclosure to all disinterested directors, or where there are none, to all shareholders, with respect to the value of property transferred or services rendered to the corporation.**

CORPORATIONS

V. MANAGEMENT OF THE CORPORATION'S AFFAIRS

A. MANAGEMENT VESTED IN BOARD OF DIRECTORS

1. **Centralized management:** Except for the following, the management of a corporation's affairs is vested in the board of directors.

   a. **Fundamental changes:** Sales of all or substantially all of the corporate assets, mergers, liquidations, and changes in the Articles of Incorporation or by-laws of the corporation ordinarily require shareholder approval.

   b. **Ratification:** The board of directors may formally adopt or implicitly ratify actions of its officers, agents, and shareholders.

   c. **Close corporations or closely held corporations:** A closely held corporation (or close corporation) is a corporation with a small number of shareholders. Those who direct the close corporation's affairs are the "managing shareholders."

2. **Benefits:** Centralized management in a board of directors has many benefits, including:

   a. It eliminates the cost of having shareholders sufficiently well informed to vote intelligently on key corporate decisions; and

   b. It avoids free-rider problems that could result if shareholders ran the corporation. For example, individuals could be tempted to shirk the responsibility of group action in the hopes that others will do the work and their benefit would therefore be greater.

B. ULTRA VIRES DOCTRINE: The board of directors is not permitted to undertake action which is beyond the corporation's authority as set forth in the Articles of Incorporation or by-laws. Under the ultra vires doctrine, a corporation cannot be obliged to undertake a contract or activity which is beyond the scope of its powers (as described in the Articles of Incorporation or by-laws).

At common law, where a contract was completely executory (i.e., neither side had begun performance of its obligations), the ultra vires doctrine could be raised by either side to the agreement as a complete defense.

Modernly, neither the corporation nor the other party to a contract can maintain an ultra vires defense, except that some states permit it to be raised by a corporation where the other party knew (or should have known) that the transaction exceeded the corporation's authority. However, in most jurisdictions, a shareholder may assert ultra vires to enjoin performance of an agreement which is beyond the scope of the corporation's authority. If warranted by the equities of the situation, an injunction may be issued. In a few states, even a shareholder cannot enjoin performance of an ultra vires agreement.

The ultra vires doctrine has little applicability today, since Articles of Incorporation typically authorize the corporation to engage in all legal activities. All that remain are activities that are illegal or which are not directed to any business purpose.

C. **CONTROVERSIAL CORPORATE ACTIVITIES**

1. **Long-term contracts:** The board of directors ordinarily has the power to bind the corporation to contracts extending beyond their term of office (unless the contract extends for an *unreasonably* lengthy period of time).

2. **Political contributions:** Contributions to the election campaigns of federal candidates are illegal, but expenditures for propositions or referenda ***cannot*** be constitutionally prohibited. These expenditures are valid as long as the contributions can reasonably be viewed as beneficial to the corporation.

3. **Charitable donations:** Reasonable charitable donations are ordinarily upheld, as long as plausible argument for long-term benefit to the corporation can be made.

D. **ELECTION/APPOINTMENT OF DIRECTORS**

1. **General rule:** The original board of directors is usually chosen by the incorporators at the initial organizational meeting. The number of directors is usually prescribed by the Articles of Incorporation or by-laws. Thereafter, directors are ordinarily elected by the shareholders at their annual meeting. If an interim vacancy occurs, the position is usually filled by vote of a majority of the board of directors.

2. **Cumulative voting:** Many states permit corporations to provide for *cumulative voting* for directors in either the Articles of Incorporation or by-laws. A few jurisdictions require cumulative voting for directors, unless the Articles of Incorporation or by-laws specifically provide otherwise.

    a. **Description:** Under cumulative voting, the shares of stock held by a shareholder are multiplied by the total number of directors to be chosen. The aggregate number of these votes can be cast ***in any manner*** the shareholder desires (e.g., all in favor of a single candidate for director, or split among any number of candidates). Under "straight" voting, each shareholder votes (or declines to vote) her total number of shares for each of the candidates. Thus cumulative voting gives minority shareholders a greater likelihood of representation on a board of directors than is possible under "straight" voting.

    b. **Example:** The Articles of Incorporation of ABC Corporation provide for the election of three directors at its annual meeting of shareholders. X owns 150 shares and Y owns 350 shares. Under straight voting, X could not elect a single member to the board of directors (i.e., Y could vote all of her 350 shares for each of the candidates whom she desired to become members of the board). Under cumulative voting, however, X has an aggregate total of 450 (150 x 3) "votes," and Y has a total of 1,050 (350 x 3) "votes." Thus, if X uses all of his 450 votes for a single director, Y cannot prevent that person's election (Y can cast 451 votes for each of two candidates, but would then have only 148 votes left).

3. **Qualifications:** The Articles of Incorporation may set out requirements for membership on the board. Absent such provision, directors generally need not own shares in the corporation nor live in the state of its incorporation.

4. **Tenure of office:** Directors usually hold their positions for one year and are elected at annual meetings of the shareholders. However, a corporation, in its Articles of Incorporation (or by-laws in some states), may provide for staggered, or classified, board. Under this system, the board is classified into groups of directors, with each group elected for a multiyear term and only one group up for reelection in any given year.

5. **Resignation, death, or removal:** If a director dies, resigns, or is removed, the Articles of Incorporation or by-laws often permit the board to appoint an interim director to serve until the next shareholders' meeting is held.

   a. **Removal without cause:** The Articles of Incorporation or by-laws usually provide for removal of a director, without cause, by a majority vote of the shareholders. However, reasonable notice must be given to the director that his removal is being sought prior to the meeting at which the vote on this issue is to be taken.

   b. **Removal for cause:** In the absence of a provision permitting removal without cause, a director can be removed by the shareholders for dishonesty, gross incompetence, or breach of his duty of loyalty to the corporation. If a director's removal for cause is being sought, he is entitled to notice of the reasons why his removal is sought and time to answer the charges against him.

   c. **Removal under cumulative voting:** Under most state statues, where cumulative voting applies for the election of directors, to prevent a majority from circumventing the will of a minority who voted for a particular director, a director cannot be removed if a minority with sufficient shares to have elected him by cumulative voting votes against his removal.

   d. **Removal by court action:** Removal by court action is possible where the directors are intentionally acting in a manner which is detrimental to the corporation (e.g., diverting assets for the benefit of a majority shareholder) and a majority of the shareholders refuse to remove the culpable individuals.

6. **"De facto" directors:** A corporation cannot repudiate a transaction it authorized by contending that the director who approved the resolution in question was not validly elected or appointed. Parties acting on the basis of a corporate resolution may ordinarily assume that the board of directors was properly constituted.

E. **HOW THE BOARD OF DIRECTORS FUNCTIONS:** Corporate powers are ordinarily exercised pursuant to express resolutions validly adopted by a majority of the board of directors at a properly called meeting. If the meeting was not properly called, or resolutions were not properly adopted, corporate action taken at the meeting, or pursuant to such resolutions may be invalid (unless subsequently *ratified* by the board).

1. **Notice of Board of Directors meeting:** An annual meeting of the board of directors is ordinarily fixed by the Articles of Incorporation or by-laws; but interim meetings can usually be called by other parties (e.g., directors, officers, or shareholders with at least 20 percent of the outstanding shares) upon proper notice. The required notice period is ordinarily set forth in the Articles of Incorporation or by-laws, or where no time has been stipulated, upon reasonable notice. Many jurisdictions permit the notice requirement to be waived in writing, either before or after the meeting. If a director who has not been properly notified is present at the meeting, the failure to give effective notice is probably waived.

2. **Quorum:** Ordinarily, only a majority (rather than all) of the directors in office must be present to constitute a quorum.

3. **Informal action:** The modern trend is to validate written resolutions signed by the requisite number of directors (without a meeting). In most jurisdictions, action by written consent of the directors must be unanimous to be valid.

4. **Ratification:** Defects in quorum, notice, or voting may be cured by postmeeting ratification (i.e., where a majority of the directors (i) sign a writing which approves the resolution, or (ii) fail to object after knowledge of the resolution is acquired).

F. **DELEGATION OF AUTHORITY BY DIRECTORS**

1. **Subcommittees:** A board of directors may ordinarily appoint subcommittees to act for it within *specified* areas. However, recommendations or decisions of these subcommittees may be overridden by the full board before they have been put into action.

2. **Provisional directors:** Provisional directors may be judicially appointed pursuant to (1) an applicable statute or (2) the Articles of Incorporation or by-laws, for the purpose of breaking deadlocks.

3. **Nondirectors:** While the performance of routine day-to-day functions may be delegated to corporate officers, "critical" or "important" management decisions (e.g., to effect a merger or a sale of all or substantially all of the corporation's assets) must be made by the board of directors.

4. **Voting agreements:** Proxies or agreements among directors to vote in a particular way with respect to prospective determinations are ordinarily void (unless a closed corporation is involved or the directors constitute *all* of the shareholders).

CORPORATIONS

G. CORPORATE OFFICERS AND AGENTS

1. **Appointment:** Major corporate officers (i.e., president, vice-presidents, secretary, and treasurer) are appointed by the board of directors. Minor officers are ordinarily appointed by the president.

2. **Removal:** Corporate officers may ordinarily be dismissed, without cause, by the board of directors.

3. **Duties:** The major corporate officers are charged with performing the following duties:

   a. **President:** The president is charged with managing the corporation's day-to-day affairs.

   b. **Vice-president:** The vice-president is ordinarily charged with performing the functions of the president when the latter is unavailable. In many jurisdictions, a vice-president may also bind the corporation to transactions which are *clearly* within the scope of its business.

   c. **Secretary:** The secretary is charged with taking minutes at director and shareholders' meetings, as well as safekeeping the corporation's books and records.

   d. **Treasurer:** The treasurer is charged with receiving, depositing, and retaining receipts for corporate income and expenditures.

4. **Authority of corporate officers and agents:** A corporation may repudiate an agreement or transaction entered into by an officer or agent who lacked proper authority. However, adequate authority will be found in the following situations:

   a. **Actual authority:** A corporate officer or agent may enter into any transaction for which he has been expressly or implicitly authorized under the Articles of Incorporation, by-laws, or a corporate resolution.

   b. **Implied authority**

      i. **Authority of office:** Corporate officers have the implied authority to enter into transactions which are reasonably related to performing the duties for which they are responsible. Thus, the president generally has the power to (1) purchase assets (i.e., equipment or inventory), (2) sell goods, used equipment, and possibly land in the ordinary course of business, (3) hire employees, and (4) establish salary levels. Similarly, a vice-president in charge of sales probably has the power to hire employees for that function.

      However, a corporate officer has no authority to (1) enter into a contract of employment which extends beyond his term of office, or, if no term is specified, the term of office of the current board of directors, (2) mortgage the corporation's assets, or (3) cause the corporation to commence bankruptcy proceedings. There is a division of authority as to whether a president can initiate litigation on behalf of the corporation.

   ii. **By custom and practice:** Where a particular corporate officer has previously entered into that type of transaction without objection by the board, she is deemed to have been impliedly authorized to bind the corporation with regard to subsequent, similar undertakings.

   iii. **By apparent authority:** Where a corporation should have recognized that a third party would be likely to view the officer or agent in question as possessing the authority to bind the corporation to the agreement in question, it cannot avoid the transaction (similar to an estoppel theory).

  c. **Ratification:** Acts of a corporate officer or agent which have not been properly authorized may be ratified by the board. Ratification may be explicit (i.e., passing a resolution which confirms the transaction) or implied (i.e., acceptance of the benefits of the agreement).

H. **COMPENSATION: Unless otherwise provided in the Articles of Incorporation or by-laws, one ordinarily receives no compensation for acting as a corporate director. However, where a director renders extraordinary services (i.e., those beyond her ordinary and usual corporate duties pursuant to a proper request), she may receive reasonable compensation for them. (Even if not specifically authorized, recovery in quasi contract may be possible, where the corporation benefited from the director's efforts.)**

Corporate officers are entitled to receive agreed-upon compensation, provided it is proper under the circumstances.

I. **INSPECTION OF CORPORATE BOOKS AND RECORDS: Directors may usually inspect their corporation's books and records. However, a court may enjoin such inspections if the director is, or would be, misusing such information (i.e., delivering customer lists to a competitor). Although some statutes state that a director's right to inspect corporate books and records is "absolute," the requirement of a "good faith purpose" may still be implied into the legislation.**

VI. RESPONSIBILITIES AND DUTIES OF CORPORATE DIRECTORS AND OFFICERS

A. **DUTY OF CARE: Directors owe a duty of care to the corporation. Directors must exercise the same degree of care and skill with respect to corporate matters as would an ordinarily prudent and diligent person with respect to his own affairs. This is essentially an antinegligence rule. With the enactment of the Sarbanes-Oxley Act of 2002, the duty of care and due diligence for directors of publicly traded companies has changed dramatically.**

CORPORATIONS

1. **Reasonable inquiry:** Directors must make a reasonable effort to apprise themselves of the facts necessary to make a proper decision. Reports furnished by corporate officers or agents may ordinarily be relied upon by directors in making their decisions.

    a. **Monitoring:** A director's duty to inquire extends only to circumstances that would alert a reasonable director.

2. **Business judgment rule:** The rule is a rebuttable presumption that directors are better equipped than courts to make business judgments and that directors are (1) disinterested, (2) reasonably diligent, and (3) acting in good faith. If these conditions are met, the directors are shielded from judicial review of, and personal liability for, their acts; if they are not, a court may review the board's acts for breach of the duty of care and hold directors personally liable.

    a. **Mere errors in business judgment are not actionable** (i.e., a director is *not* a guarantor of corporate financial success).

        i. **Policy arguments in favor of the business judgment rule**

            (a) **Institutional competence:** Courts do not have the business expertise of a board of directors, which is intimately familiar with the corporation's affairs.

            (b) **Cost savings:** Judicial review is costly.

            (c) **Promotion of innovation and risk taking:** Intervention by courts leads to defensive moves and has a chilling effect. The business judgment rule, which allows for confidence in the board of directors, promotes innovation and risk taking.

            (d) **Encourages well-qualified persons to serve:** The business judgement rule encourages well-qualified persons to serve as directors by insulating them from liability for the business risks they take on behalf of the corporation. In other words, even if a decision made by the board, but in the exercise of its business judgment, turns out to be a bad one, a court will not judge that decision in hindsight.

            (e) **Other remedies are available:** Other measures, such as the market for corporate control (i.e., poorly run corporations are particularly vulnerable to takeovers), removal of the board and/or individual board members, and incentives tied to stock price are available to discipline the board's decision making.

            (f) **Protection of the shareholders:** Too much judicial scrutiny ultimately undoes the system of centralized management. The business judgment rule therefore protects the shareholders from themselves.

OUTLINE

b. **Directors are not entitled to the presumption of the business judgment rule** when their actions (1) are fraudulent, illegal, or motivated by personal interest (all instances of a lack of good faith); (2) lack a rational business purpose (i.e., they constitute a waste of corporate assets); or (3) are grossly negligent and uninformed.

3. **Defenses**

   a. **Nonparticipation or dissent:** Directors who dissented or failed to participate in the negligent corporate action are ordinarily *not* liable (unless they should have undertaken more forceful steps to prevent or terminate the conduct in question).

   b. **Shareholder ratification:** Where the shareholders unanimously ratify the unreasonable conduct, no action can be maintained.

   c. **Nondefenses:** Where disabled or nonresident directors voted for the unreasonable conduct in question, or failed to take steps to prevent or terminate the questionable conduct after it had commenced, their personal difficulties in keeping apprised of corporate affairs is ordinarily not an excuse.

   d. **Exculpation:** Most states have passed statutes that authorize corporations, via shareholder-adopted charter amendments, to shield directors from personal liability for breaching the duty of care.

4. **Oversight under Sarbanes-Oxley:** In 2002, in response to perceived failures of corporate oversight at Enron and other corporations, Congress passed the Sarbanes-Oxley Act. In addition to mandating stricter standards for accounting firms retained by "reporting companies" (those whose shares are publicly traded, thereby requiring them to file periodic reports with the SEC), Sarbanes-Oxley put in place several new requirements intended to enhance oversight at reporting companies. Principal among them are rules mandating:

   a. **Corporate responsibility for financial reports:** Under new SEC rules adopted in accordance with Sarbanes-Oxley, the CEO and CFO of reporting companies (the "signing officers") must certify, for each annual and quarterly report their company files with the SEC, that they have reviewed the report; that the report does not contain any material untrue statements, material omissions, or is otherwise misleading; and that the financial statements fairly present the financial condition and results of the company in all material respects. A knowing failure to fully comply with these requirements carries penalties of up to $1 million and 10 years in prison, and willful violations up to $5 million and 20 years in prison.

   b. **Internal controls:** Sarbanes-Oxley also mandates reporting companies to establish internal controls and procedures to ensure that corporate officers are

CORPORATIONS

made aware of all material financial information subject to disclosure under SEC rules. Signing officers must certify in their company's SEC annual and quarterly reports that they are responsible for internal controls and have evaluated their effectiveness within the previous 90 days, and must give management's assessment of the effectiveness of the company's internal controls. Any deficiencies in the controls or significant changes that could have a negative impact on them must be reported, as well as any fraud involving employees with responsibility for internal activities.

   c. **Whistleblower protection:** Sarbanes-Oxley protects employee whistleblowers by requiring reporting companies to establish procedures to allow employees to submit information regarding "questionable accounting or auditing matters" anonymously. Further, Sarbanes-Oxley forbids and punishes retaliation against employee whistleblowers.

   d. **Audit committee:** Under new stock exchange rules mandated by Sarbanes-Oxley, a reporting company's audit committee must be made up entirely of independent directors, with at least one of them having, and disclosed as having, "significant auditing, accounting, financial, or other comparable experience." The audit committee, rather than the entire board, under Sarbanes-Oxley, must be solely responsible for the hiring, compensation, and oversight of the company's independent auditors.

   e. **Code of ethics:** To encourage reporting companies to adopt codes of ethics—written standards designed to deter wrongdoing and encourage ethical, honest conduct, including the ethical handling of conflicts of interest, and full and accurate disclosure in company reports—binding on corporate officers, Sarbanes-Oxley requires reporting companies to disclose if they have adopted such a code of ethics, and if not, to explain why they have not done so.

B. **DUTY OF LOYALTY: Directors owe a duty of loyalty to the corporation obligating them to put corporate interests ahead of their own. Of particular concern are transactions in which a director arguably usurps a corporate opportunity, or otherwise competes with the corporation, and self-dealing transactions, where a director and the corporation are parties to transaction, such that the director potentially is on both sides, approving a transaction, as a director, for the corporation that benefits her personally.**

   1. **Corporate opportunity doctrine:** A director or officer cannot exploit information or opportunities, acquired or made available to him as a consequence of his corporate position, for personal gain, unless the corporation (i) after full disclosure declines to pursue the opportunity, or (ii) is, and would continue to be by any reasonable efforts, clearly unable to exploit the opportunity.

      a. **Description of corporate opportunity:** There is no clear definition of what constitutes a corporate opportunity. It is any transaction or property in which the corporation had, or would be likely to have, an interest in pursuing at the time the "opportunity" was appropriated.

b. **Tests:** Courts have employed a number of tests to determine whether a corporate opportunity exists.

   i. **Line of Business:** The corporation has a prior claim to a business opportunity presented to a director if it falls within the company's line of business, which can extend beyond the corporation's existing operations.

   ii. **Fairness:** Fairness to the corporation is always a defense. A director has not breached his duty of loyalty if he has acted fairly.

   iii. **Interest or expectancy:** Whether or not the corporation would have been interested in taking the opportunity and has the current financial ability to do so.

   iv. **Combination of line of business and fairness:** Courts will sometimes combine these two tests to determine whether a director has unfairly taken an opportunity rightfully and reasonably seen as within the business of the corporation.

   v. **Interest or expectancy:** Courts will examine whether the corporation has a present interest or tangible expectancy in the sense that it has a specific need for the opportunity, has resolved to acquire such an opportunity, or has actively considered its acquisition.

c. **Remedies:** The corporation can assert whatever equitable (i.e., a mandatory injunction requiring the director or officer to transfer the property to it, imposing a constructive trust upon the asset, etc.) or legal remedies are available to make the culpable party disgorge his profit or advantage.

2. **Conflict of interest situations:** Where a director or officer has a direct financial interest in a transaction, he is ordinarily obliged to make full disclosure of his interest and refrain from voting on that matter. Such a transaction is not void or voidable solely because of a director's interest in the transaction if (1) the material facts of the director's interest are fully disclosed to the board and, the transaction is approved by a majority of *__disinterested directors,__* or (2) the material facts of the director's interest are fully disclosed to the shareholders and the transaction is approved by a majority of the *__disinterested shareholders,__* or (3) a court determines the transaction to be fair. If conditions (1) or (2) are not met and the transaction is challenged in court, the burden is on the board to prove the entire fairness of the transaction to the corporation and its shareholders. If those conditions are met and the transaction is challenged, the burden of proving entire fairness shifts to the plaintiff challenging the transaction.

   a. **Valid quorum:** There is a division of authority as to whether interested directors are counted in determining if there was a valid quorum to consider the matter.

   b. **Interested director:** A director is *__not disinterested__* if he is under the influence or control of the person affected by the transaction (i.e., a disinterested director must also be "independent").

CORPORATIONS

      c. **Interlocking directorships:** Where someone is a director of two different corporations which are transacting business with each other, he is ordinarily obliged to disclose this conflict.

      d. **Entire fairness:** Courts have held that entire fairness has both substantive and procedural components. Substantive fairness concerns whether the transaction is at a "fair price"—within the range of what a market transaction negotiated at arm's length would have generated. Procedural fairness concerns whether the director's interest in the transaction was properly disclosed, the process followed for approving the transaction, and the interested director's role in that process.

      e. **Remedy:** If feasible, the *corporation* may rescind the transaction if it is challenged and found not to have been entirely fair. If this is not practicable, the corporation can recover any damages or losses which it incurred by entering into the transaction from the interested director.

   3. **Competition with one's own corporation:** Directors and (in some states) officers are not automatically disqualified from serving the corporation if they engaged in a competing business. However, if a director or officer uses his corporate position, in any manner, to gain a competitive advantage, he is liable for all losses or damages resulting to the corporation. An officer or director is not required to disclose plans to commence a competing business prior to resigning from the corporation. However, he may *not* solicit key personnel of the corporation prior to resigning.

C. **EXECUTIVE COMPENSATION:** Today corporate executives are compensated in a number of ways. As direct compensation, they receive salaries and bonuses for their services to the corporation, as well as stock grants and stock options as incentives for executive performance, aligning their financial interests directly with their shareholders', and pension plans and other deferred compensation. Indirect compensation, in the form of fringe benefits, expense accounts, can also be quite lucrative for corporate executives.

   1. **Approval:** When executive compensation is approved by disinterested directors, it is only subject to business judgment review, meaning it can only be challenged successfully by proving the disinterested directors were grossly uninformed when they approved the compensation or the compensation constitutes a waste of corporate assets. In such a challenge, courts typically give great deference to the disinterested and independent approval of executive compensation.

   2. **Past services:** To the extent that a director, officer, or employee is compensated for *past* services (i.e., via a bonus, retirement benefits, or a pension), the compensation *may* be voidable. However, some jurisdictions take the view that the corporation obtains a present benefit, since present members of the corporation will be inspired to greater loyalty by these actions.

   3. **Fairness review:** If challenged, executive compensation that has not been approved by informed, disinterested, independent directors (or by a majority

of informed, disinterested shareholders) is subject to fairness review. Whether compensation is fair and reasonable or not is determined by a variety of circumstances, such as

   a. the magnitude of the corporation's operations,

   b. the compensation paid to persons performing comparable services for other corporations,

   c. the amount of time and energy necessary to perform corporate responsibilities,

   d. the potential liability which could be incurred as a result of the responsibility which has been assumed, and

   e. the experience and expertise of the recipient of the compensation.

   4. **Future services:** Compensation for future services may be voidable if not explicitly conditioned upon remaining with the corporation for an appropriate period of time.

D. **REACQUISITION OF SHARES:** Where directors repurchase stock of their corporation with its funds *for the purpose of perpetuating their control,* they have breached their fiduciary obligation to the shareholders and are liable to the corporation for wasting corporate funds. However, where the directors' action was motivated by a desire to prevent the looting of corporate assets or the corporation's operations from being undermined, their actions are proper.

E. **ACQUISITION OF CORPORATE DEBT:** Assuming no violation of the corporate opportunity doctrine, a director may acquire and enforce an outstanding claim against the corporation. However, where the obligation is, or could be, disputed by the corporation, the interested director is obliged to disclose his interest and refrain from any discussions pertaining to that debt.

F. **DISTRIBUTION OF DIVIDENDS:** A corporation's ability to declare dividends is within the business discretion of the directors. However, the failure to make distributions for personal reasons (e.g., to freeze out particular shareholders, to avoid the imposition of individual taxes, etc.) violates the fiduciary duty of good faith owed to the stockholders. Conversely, directors are liable to the corporation for delivering and distributing an *improper* dividend.

VII. SHAREHOLDERS

A. **VOTING:** While shareholders have no direct voice in the management of their corporation, they can influence corporate management by voting for the election or removal of directors. In addition, shareholders vote on major corporate changes entrusted to them by law (mergers, sales of all or substantially all of the corporation's assets) or under the Articles of Incorporation, and they can, on a

CORPORATIONS

limited basis, bring up matters of corporate reform and policy for consideration at shareholder meetings.

1. **Shareholder meetings:** An annual shareholders' meeting is ordinarily prescribed by the Articles of Incorporation or by-laws. Special interim meetings can usually be called by the board of directors, officers, or shareholders with a prescribed proportion (ordinarily, at least 10 percent) of the corporation's stock. Most special meetings are called when a shareholder vote is needed to approve a major corporate transaction.

   a. **Notice:** Notice of the annual meeting need only indicate the date, time, and place where it will be held. However, notice of a special meeting must also indicate the matters to be voted upon. (Even regular meetings require notice of extraordinary business determinations.)

   b. **Quorum requirements:** Ordinarily, persons representing a majority of the outstanding shares as of the "record date" (i.e., a date designated prior to the meeting) must be present, either in person or by proxy. While there is a division of authority, the majority view is that once a quorum is present, it does not cease to exist because persons holding the necessary shares or proxies leave the meeting.

2. **Voting:** Except as already discussed with respect to cumulative voting for directors, shareholders ordinarily have one vote per each share held. A minority (but increasing number) of states permits shareholder actions to be undertaken without a meeting, via written consent, where (1) there is unanimous agreement among the shareholders, or (2) reasonable prior notice is given to all of the shareholders about the proposed action.

   a. **Higher than "majority vote" requirements:** The Articles of Incorporation or by-laws sometimes prescribe greater than majority requirements for a quorum or specific corporate action (e.g., 75 percent of the shares entitled to vote at a meeting required to approve a merger). However, provisions requiring unanimity are ordinarily void, since there is little flexibility to adapt to changing economic circumstances.

   b. **Voting by proxy:** Through a proxy, a shareholder gives another person the right to exercise the shareholder's voting rights. The proxy usually must be in writing. For "public" companies—those whose securities are registered under the Securities Exchange Act of 1934 (the "Exchange Act")—any proxy solicitation made must comply with SEC rules promulgated under Section 14 of the Exchange Act. Under the proxy rules, emphasis is on disclosure, to ensure that public investors have adequate information.

      i. **Prohibited Conduct:** Section 14(a) of the Exchange Act makes the solicitation of any proxy in violation of SEC rules unlawful.

ii. **Definition:** SEC Rule 14a-1 gives "proxy" the broadest possible definition consistent with the statute. A proxy need not be a physical piece of paper, and a shareholder's oral consent may be sufficient.

iii. **Disclosure:** SEC Rule 14a-3 requires that certain things be disclosed to shareholders in connection with proxy solicitations, including conflict of interest, management remuneration, and details of major corporate changes that are to be voted on. SEC Rule 14a-5 creates an important relaxation of disclosure requirements. Information which is "not known to the persons on whose behalf the solicitation is to be made and which is not reasonably within the power of such persons to ascertain or procure may be omitted, if a brief statement of the circumstances rendering such information unavailable is made."

iv. **Solicitation:** SEC Rule 14a-7 requires that, if management intends to make a proxy solicitation, the corporation must (a) also mail out proxy materials supplied by a shareholder that deal with the same subject matter (the shareholder must pay any reasonable additional expense of the mailing); or (b) provide the shareholder with the shareholder list for mailing his solicitation to shareholders. Generally corporations are reluctant to provide shareholders with a shareholder list for proxy solicitations, as the list could readily be used for purposes other than the shareholder's proxy solicitation—such as a corporate takeover.

v. **Revocation:** A shareholder who has granted a proxy may revoke it in several ways: by notifying the person given the proxy, by giving it to another person, or by the shareholder's personal attendance and vote at a shareholders' meeting. A shareholder can usually revoke his proxy at any time, unless he has coupled it with an interest in shares and expressly stated that it is irrevocable.

vi. **Shareholder proposals:** Under SEC Rule 14a-8, any shareholder owning at least one percent or $1000 in market value of securities may submit a proposal for consideration at the shareholders' meeting. The proposal must be in the form of a resolution that the shareholder intends to present at the meeting. Shareholder proposals must be timely submitted, usually at least 120 calendar days before the meeting. If the proposal is proper (see exceptions below) management must include it in the corporation's proxy mailing to shareholders. A shareholder proposal, with an accompanying supporting statement, cannot exceed 500 words, and management's proxy card must give shareholders an opportunity to vote for or against the proposal.

(a) **Exceptions:** Management may omit any proposal for any number of reasons, including if it is for a political cause, that is, not related to the company's business or not within its power to effectuate. The rule, however, does not necessarily exclude social-issue proposals. Management may also omit proposals relating to operations that account for less than five percent of the corporation's total assets and less than five percent of its net earnings and sales, as well as if it is related to ordinary business operations.

vii. **Shareholder suits:** SEC Rule 14a-9, an antifraud provision, outlaws false and misleading statements and omissions with respect to any material fact in connection with proxy solicitations. In a private suit challenging a proxy solicitation on these grounds, the plaintiff must show culpability and materiality. A false or misleading statement will not give rise to a private right of action unless it was the cause of the shareholder vote. It is unsettled if the plaintiff must prove scienter (i.e., management's knowingly making a false or misleading statement or omission). However, many jurisdictions hold that a showing of negligence is sufficient. Also, a plaintiff need not prove actual reliance; if the plaintiff establishes materiality, causation is normally presumed. Remedies for violation of Rule 14a-9 include recission, injunction, or damages. Availability of remedies, however, hinges on the fairness of the transaction; if the transaction was fair, the plaintiff cannot obtain damages.

c. **Pooling agreements:** Under a pooling agreement, two or more shareholders agree to vote their shares as all (or a majority) of them decide. This device is ordinarily used by minority shareholders to marshal the aggregate number of votes necessary to veto corporate action of which they disapprove. In a pooling agreement, the participants retain legal title to their shares (even though they have promised to vote their shares as the majority decides). Where, in the context of a pooling agreement, a proxy has not been issued to an agent for the purpose of voting the group's shares, the arrangement can be enforced through a specific performance decree. Where a proxy has been issued to an agent, most (but not all) courts hold it to be irrevocable (i.e., the power to vote constitutes a sufficient "interest"). A few states refuse to enforce pooling agreements, unless *all* of the shareholders involved are parties to the action.

d. **Voting trusts:** Under a voting trust, shareholders assign their legal interest in the shares to a trustee, for which the shareholders receive a trust certificate as evidence of the interest. The trustee is instructed to vote the shares in a prescribed manner. One of the trustee's duties is to remit dividends to the shareholders in accordance with the proportions shown by the trust certificates. Unless a voting trust is specific as to extraordinary matters (sale of substantially all of the assets, dissolution, merger, etc.), the trustee will *not* be permitted to vote the shares assigned to him. However, as to nonmaterial actions which are *not* covered by the agreement, the trustee is ordinarily authorized to vote the shares in the manner which he believes the shareholders would have desired.

e. **Revocability and enforceability of pooling agreements and voting trusts:** Pooling agreements and voting trusts may always be revoked by unanimous vote of the shareholder-participants. Many jurisdictions have legislation pertaining to voting trusts. Failure to comply with these statutes can result in the agreement being unenforceable. Modernly, however, some courts uphold the agreement, unless the failure to comply with statutory requirements is material. Voting trusts and sometimes pooling agreements must be filed with the corporation and open to inspection by prospective shareholders. If this is not done, the agreement may be invalid.

f. **Proxy contests:** Proxy contests occur when an organized opposition mounts a campaign against corporate insiders (management and/or the board).

   i. **Types**

      (a) **Control contest:** Control contests are fights over control of the board.

      (b) **Issue contest:** Issue contests involve votes on a fundamental corporate change that requires shareholder approval.

   ii. **Benefits of proxy contests:** Proxy fights have become a popular venue for change, as insiders cannot block them as easily as they can block takeover attempts. Other benefits to shareholders can include:

   (a) A new and better board of directors;

   (b) An increased share price upon the announcement of a proxy fight;

   (c) A disciplinary effect on the board ex ante (the mere possibility of a proxy fight can make a board more responsive).

   iii. **Reimbursement:** Ideally, the law would encourage good proxy fights and discourage bad ones. Not only is this a difficult goal to achieve, but the law currently does not provide for reimbursement to shareholder-sponsored proxy fights as a matter of right.

      (a) **Insiders:** Directors may reimburse themselves from the corporate treasury for "reasonable" expenses associated with a proxy contest where the contest is over policy (not over personal power).

      (b) **Insurgents:** Unlike management, insurgents do not have a right to reimbursement for proxy fight expenses, even if they win. Successful insurgents *may* be reimbursed from corporate funds for expenses incurred in a proxy fight, provided that (1) reimbursement is ratified by a majority of shareholders; (2) the contest is over corporate policy and not for personal control; and (3) the expenses are reasonable both in nature and amount.

(c) **Is this unequal treatment good?** Yes and no.

   (1) Full reimbursement for incumbents means that they can spend heavy sums, driving up costs and making it more difficult for non-incumbents to win.

   (2) It can be good if we think that incumbents have already shown their worth by virtue of the fact that they are in power, and, as such, deserve to have an edge.

(d) **What if reimbursement were contingent on success?**

   (1) A rule that makes reimbursement contingent on success discourages bad proxy fights.

   (2) Such a rule also discourages good proxy fights, since there is no guarantee that the proxy fight will succeed.

   (3) One idea is that, in order to compensate an insurgent for the risk of initiating a proxy fight, he could be paid a multiple of his expenses, the multiple based on the frequency of successful investigations. Practically, however, it would be difficult to achieve this system.

(e) **Reimbursement only for control contests:** Some jurisdictions, including Delaware, allow shareholders to recover proxy contest costs only in successful control contests and not in successful issue contests.

   (1) **Reason:** Because the corporation is not obligated to compensate, the insurgents need to gain control in order to get reimbursed.

   (2) **Critique:** It can be argued that there is a greater need for reimbursement in issue contests, because the insurgent does not gain the private benefits of control and because it is more likely in an issue contest that he is motivated by the share price rather than by personal gain.

B. **PREEMPTIVE RIGHTS**

   1. **Common law rule:** Where there is a *new issuance of shares*, an existing shareholder has a right (but not an obligation) to acquire the shares necessary to maintain her present, proportionate interest in the corporation. This right, however, must be exercised in a reasonably prompt manner.

   2. **Modern rule:** No preemptive rights exist, unless so provided for in the Articles of Incorporation or by-laws. Few corporations provide for preemptive rights for all shareholders because such rights may unduly restrict the corporation's ability to raise capital. It is not uncommon, however, for corporations to grant preemptive rights to purchasers of preferred stock (particularly venture capital investors).

OUTLINE

3. **Nonapplicability:** *Preemptive rights do not apply to*:

   a. The issuance of stock which had already been authorized when the aggrieved party acquired her shares,

   b. The reissuance of treasury stock,

   c. Shares issued by the corporation for services or property, and

   d. The issuance of other classes of stock.

4. **Equitable considerations:** Even where preemptive rights are **not** recognized or are not applicable, many courts will disallow the issuance of new shares, or permit "quasi" preemptive rights, where directors or majority shareholders are seeking to (i) dilute the interest of earlier shareholders, or (ii) take unfair advantage of minority shareholders. In these instances, the directors or majority shareholders are in violation of their fiduciary duties to the minority stockholders.

5. **Remedies:** Where preemptive rights are violated, a court may:

   a. Decree equitable relief (i.e., enjoin the corporation from selling the shares in question or order the new purchaser to transfer his shares to the aggrieved shareholder), or

   b. Award damages (the difference between the (i) book, or (ii) fair market value of the shares to which the aggrieved shareholder would have been entitled, and the issuance price of those shares).

C. **RIGHT TO RECEIVE DIVIDENDS**

1. **Description of dividends:** Dividends are distributions, either in the form of cash or property (ordinarily, additional stock) made by a corporation to its shareholders in proportion to their ownership of outstanding stock. Unless management is failing to act in good faith, the board of directors cannot be compelled to issue dividends. In most states, no dividends are allowed where the distributions would cause the corporation to (1) become insolvent (i.e., be unable to satisfy its obligations as they become due, or result in its total liabilities exceeding its total assets), or (2) be unable to make required payments due to holders of preferred shares.

2. **When dividends may be paid:** Ordinarily, dividends can be paid *only* from a corporation's "surplus." Surplus is the difference between a corporation's net assets (total assets, minus total liabilities, for the applicable accounting period) and its "stated capital." Stated capital (which is designated under the "capital stock" account within the corporate ledger) is the aggregate amount received by the corporation for the shares of stock it has issued and outstanding. There are several ways in which a surplus can be achieved:

   a. **Earned surplus:** The corporation's **total** assets exceed **its total** liabilities (including stated capital).

CORPORATIONS

b. **Capital reduction surplus:** The surplus resulting when par value stock (or the stated value of "no par" value stock is involved) is reduced. This reduction can be accomplished only pursuant to (i) a validly passed resolution, (ii) the consent of the requisite number of shareholders (ordinarily, two-thirds or three-quarters), or the filing of an amendment reflecting the change in the value of the stock with the proper state authority (usually the secretary of state).

c. **Paid-in surplus:** The surplus resulting when the corporation has (1) issued par value shares for an amount in excess of par, (2) issued no par stock for an amount in excess of its stated value, or (3) received gifts.

d. **Revaluation (sometimes called "reappraisal") surplus:** The surplus resulting when a corporation upwardly revalues its assets, so that their aggregate value exceeds their original cost or (if received by the corporation for the stock) valuation. (There is a division of authority as to whether revaluation surplus may be used as a source of dividends.)

3. **Nimble dividends:** A few states permit the payment of "nimble" dividends (i.e., dividends which are permissible, despite the fact that a *surplus does not exist at the time distribution is made*). Some jurisdictions permit dividends to be paid as long as the distributions can be made from net operating profits. Others permit nimble dividends as long as the total assets exceed total liabilities (exclusive of the corporation's stated capital).

4. **Record date:** In the resolution authorizing payment of dividends, it is ordinarily stated that recipients will be the shareholders of record as of a specific date.

    a. If stock is transferred *prior* to the designated date, and this change is not indicated in the stock register, the corporation may (without liability) make distribution to the shareholder shown of record on the designated date (unless the corporation has delayed an unreasonably lengthy period of time in changing the stock register subsequent to receiving notice of the transfer).

    b. If no date of distribution is specified, the dividend may be paid (without liability to the corporation) to the record owner of the shares on the date that the dividend was declared.

5. **Irrevocability of dividends:** Once a dividend is declared, it cannot ordinarily be rescinded by the corporation (unless subsequent payment of the dividend would impair the corporation's ability to operate or would be improper). *Stock dividends*, however, may be cancelled prior to issuance of the shares.

6. **Consequences of an improper dividend**

    a. **Directors:** Directors who, as a consequence of a lack of good faith or failure to exercise reasonable business judgment, do not object to an improper dividend are jointly and severally liable to shareholders to the extent it can be shown that the distribution impaired the corporation's ability to operate.

b. **Shareholders:** Shareholders who are unaware that a dividend which they receive is improper ordinarily have no liability for that distribution to the corporation's creditors. However, in some jurisdictions, recovery from shareholders can be obtained by creditors where the corporation was *insolvent* when the distribution was made. Additionally, where a shareholder was aware that the dividend she received was *not proper*, directors can usually obtain indemnity from them to the extent they have liability to the creditors (but in no event can this right to indemnity exceed the improper dividend received by a shareholder).

D. **DERIVATIVE ACTIONS**

1. **Nature of action:** A derivative action is an action in which the shareholder sues on behalf of the corporation. A derivative action is appropriate where the harm complained of was done *primarily* to the corporation (rather than to the plaintiff/shareholder). If a derivative action is successful, the recovery (other than attorney's fees) must be paid directly to the corporation.

    a. In a direct action (vs. a derivative action), the shareholder may sue the corporate fiduciaries either as individuals or as part of a class action, with the recovery going to the suing shareholders.

2. **Procedural requisites**

    a. **Contemporaneous ownership of stock:** The plaintiff must have been a shareholder (a registered or equitable owner) when the harm to the corporation allegedly occurred. Additionally, courts sometimes bar a board of directors which was elected by a person who became a shareholder *after* the alleged harm occurred from commencing an action against the alleged wrongdoer.

    A plaintiff who was *not* a shareholder at the time of the alleged wrong may commence a derivative action in the following situations:

    i. The plaintiff acquired her shares through operation of law (i.e., inheritance),

    ii. The derivative action is premised upon SEC Rule 16(b) under the Exchange Act, which prohibits "short-swing" profits on purchases and sales of stock within six months of each other, or

    iii. A substantial injustice will occur unless the action is permitted.

    b. **Demand upon directors:** A shareholder must ordinarily demand that the board of directors commence the action to redress the alleged wrongs, unless it would obviously be futile to do so (i.e., all, or a majority, of the directors are the purported wrongdoers).

    i. Where (i) the demand to sue is refused by the board in good faith and in the exercise of their reasonable business judgment, and (ii) it is *not* alleged that the directors are personally at fault, the action ordinarily cannot be pursued.

ii. Where a minority of the board is accused of wrongdoing, a derivative action is sometimes barred where (i) a majority of the disinterested directors, in good faith and in the exercise of their reasonable business judgment, decline to pursue the action, or (ii) an independent "litigation" committee of disinterested directors determines that it would *not* be in the corporation's interest to pursue the action.

iii. If the board accedes to the demand, then the corporation assumes control of the litigation and the shareholder is precluded from bringing suit.

iv. The justifications most often given for the demand requirement are:

(a) **Furthering centralized management:** The decision on whether or not to sue is a function of the business judgment rule.

(b) **Judicial economy:** Some suits may be avoided.

(c) **Protecting directors from harassment:** Without the demand requirement, some shareholders might be tempted to challenge ordinary business decisions.

(d) **Discouraging "strike suits":** The demand requirement can discourage suits based on reckless charges and brought for personal gain.

c. **Demand upon shareholders:** In many states, the plaintiff must also request the shareholders to ratify or approve the derivative action. If a majority of disinterested shareholders decline to approve the action, it is barred.

i. Where the derivative action is premised upon illegal acts by the directors which have caused injury or loss to the corporation, shareholder approval is unnecessary (i.e., the wrongful action *cannot* be ratified).

ii. Where the derivative action is based upon (i) an alleged failure to conform to the business judgment rule, or (ii) engagement in acts which require shareholder approval, shareholder approval must ordinarily be obtained.

Some states dispense with the requirement of shareholder approval where the cost would be prohibitive.

d. **Security for expenses:** In many states, the plaintiff must post a bond or deposit other security with the court sufficient to indemnify the corporation against attorneys' fees and litigation expenses in the event the derivative action is unsuccessful. In a few jurisdictions, this requirement is waived where the plaintiff owns a specified percentage or dollar value of the outstanding stock.

i. Where the corporation has indemnified the officers or directors accused of wrongdoing, the security posted by the plaintiff must also be sufficient to cover the attorneys' fees and litigation expenses of those persons.

ii. In some jurisdictions, recourse against the security is permitted only if the court finds that the unsuccessful action was brought "without reasonable cause."

e. **Independent committees:** Where a suit alleges wrongdoing by a majority of directors, the board may appoint a special committee of disinterested directors to investigate the claim and recommend action. Courts in most jurisdictions pay deference to such a committee's recommendations.

3. **Settlement or dismissal:** Settlement or dismissal of a derivative action must ordinarily be approved by the court (after notice to the shareholders).

    a. Notice of the proposed dismissal or settlement must usually be given to shareholders.

    b. Dismissal or settlement of a derivative action is ordinarily res judicata as to the claims asserted in that suit. Thus, other shareholders of the corporation are barred from commencing similar litigation.

4. **Equitable defenses:** Since a derivative action is equitable in nature, equitable defenses (i.e., laches, pari delicto, unclean hands, etc.) can be asserted by a defendant.

5. **Consequences of litigation**

    a. If successful, the plaintiff is entitled to reimbursement from the corporation for his reasonable attorneys' fees and litigation expenses. The balance of the recovery, however, is remitted directly to the corporation (except where this procedure would benefit shareholders who should not be permitted to share in the recovery).

    b. If the defendants are successful,

        i. Further litigation based upon the underlying action is barred under res judicata principles, and

        ii. The plaintiff must pay for the defendant's costs of litigation and, in some jurisdictions, the latter's attorneys' fees may also be awarded.

6. **Indemnification of directors or officers**

    a. **Defendant successful on merits:** Where the defendant (who is a director or officer) is successful on the merits, most states permit the corporation to indemnify him for attorneys' fees and litigation expenses incurred in defending the action.

CORPORATIONS

   b. **Pretrial settlement:** Where the action is settled prior to judgment, most jurisdictions permit the corporation to indemnify the defendant for his attorneys' fees and litigation expenses, provided a majority of the disinterested directors or shareholders consider the defendant to have been acting in good faith (even where the settlement includes a payment by the defendant to the corporation).

E. **TRANSFERABILITY OF SHARES**

 1. **General rule:** A shareholder may transfer his stock, subject to reasonable restrictions upon alienability. These restrictions may be found in the Articles of Incorporation, by-laws, or in shareholder agreements. If the restriction is contained in a shareholder agreement, a conspicuous reference to the restriction must be printed or otherwise shown on the shares themselves.

 2. **Reasonable restrictions:** Restrictions which are usually upheld include:

   a. Giving the corporation a right of first refusal,

   b. Compelling the sale of shares for a predetermined amount (even if lower than the market or book value) upon (i) the death of a shareholder, or (ii) his ceasing to be employed by the corporation, and

   c. Prohibiting sales to particular types of persons (e.g., competitors).

 3. **Unreasonable restrictions:** Restrictions which have been invalidated include:

   a. Requiring a sale or transfer to be approved by a majority of the shareholders or board of directors (a few states accept such restrictions, but imply "good faith" into the determination of the applicable body), and

   b. Prohibiting sales to specific racial or ethnic groups.

 4. **Strict interpretation:** Restrictions relating to the transferability of stock are ordinarily interpreted strictly (i.e., provisions limiting "transfers or sales" to only members of the corporation have been construed as applying to only ***voluntary transfers***, rather than to transfers which occur as a result of inheritance or foreclosure upon a pledge of the stock).

 5. **Subsequent limitations on transferability:** Shares issued prior to the time that a corporation places a restriction upon them are ordinarily not subject to that limitation. However, in a few states, where a shareholder votes in favor of a particular restriction, his shares are deemed to be covered by that restraint (even though his stock was issued prior to that time).

 6. **Remedies**

   a. **Against the shareholder:** If a shareholder wrongfully transfers stock to a bona fide purchaser, the corporation can obtain damages from the former (but has no action against the latter).

b. **Against the transferee:** The corporation is not obliged to acknowledge the acquisition of shares by someone who accepted them with knowledge that a restriction prevented their transferability to him.

F. **INSPECTION OF CORPORATE BOOKS AND RECORDS**

1. **Common law rule:** A shareholder ordinarily has the right to inspect corporate books and records, provided she has a ***proper purpose*** (i.e., advancing the corporation's interests in some manner) in doing so.

    a. **Burden of proof/common law:** At common law, the shareholder usually had the burden of proving that his purpose was proper.

    b. **Burden of proof/modern statutes:** Many states have enacted statutes which shift the burden of proving why the shareholder should not be allowed to inspect the corporation's books and records where certain circumstances are present (e.g., the shareholder owns at least five percent of the outstanding shares, she has been a shareholder for at least six months, etc.).

2. **Proper Purpose:** Examples of proper purposes to inspect corporate books and records include:

    a. Obtaining stockholder names and addresses to solicit proxies, where the shareholder believes in good faith that the policies of the present board are ineffective.

    b. Where the shareholder seeking the information is considering the sale of her stock, obtaining the data necessary to determine the proper price per share.

    c. Investigating possible mismanagement where evidence justifies concern.

    d. Determining the reason for nonpayment of dividends.

3. **Improper purpose:** Examples of an improper purpose to inspect corporate books and records include:

    a. Seeking the information to furnish it to a business competitor, or

    b. Obtaining the data to promote the shareholder's personal, social, or political concerns.

4. **Statutory interpretation of inspection statutes:** Where a statute pertaining to the rights of shareholders to inspect corporate books and records exists, it is usually narrowly construed to permit assertion of common law rights (i.e., where a statute permits only shareholders with at least five percent of the corporation's stock to inspect the annual ***balance sheet,*** a shareholder with less than this percentage can still assert her common law rights to view the ***shareholder lists***).

CORPORATIONS

5. **Section 14(a) rights:** If a solicitation for proxies made by the board of directors is subject to Section 14(a) of the Exchange Act, shareholders of the corporation have a *right* to demand a list of shareholders entitled to vote. If this demand is refused, the board of directors *must* mail the shareholder's proxy materials with its own (but the shareholder must pay any increased postage resulting from including his materials).

VIII. FIDUCIARY OBLIGATIONS OF MAJORITY OR CONTROLLING SHAREHOLDERS

A. **GENERAL RULE:** Majority or controlling shareholders of a corporation have a fiduciary duty to refrain from exercising their position in a manner which takes undue advantage or oppresses the minority shareholders.

B. **EXAMPLES:** Examples of improper conduct include the following:

1. Causing the board of directors to guarantee loans made to, or to enter into loans with, a majority shareholder,

2. Causing the board of directors to issue additional stock for the purpose of diluting the minority's interest,

3. Causing the board of directors to enter into contracts with the majority shareholder (or an entity affiliated with him) on unusually favorable terms, or

4. Causing the board of directors to dissolve the corporation, or sell its assets, for the purpose of excluding the minority shareholders from participation in a profitable business.

C. **FREEZE-OUTS:** A freeze-out occurs when a controlling shareholder wishes to eliminate ("freeze out") minority shareholders. The most common freeze-out technique is for the controlling shareholder to issue cash, rather than stock, in exchange for the stock of the disappearing corporation in a merger. Since approval by majority of shareholders binds all shareholders, minority shareholders must either accept the consideration offered or exercise their appraisal rights. A freeze-out may be permissible if for a legitimate business purpose, and in some states, is subject to judicial review for "entire fairness" (fair dealing and fair price) to the minority shareholders.

D. **SHAREHOLDERS IN CLOSE CORPORATIONS:** In a close corporation, *all* shareholders owe each other an even stricter duty than that is owed by controlling shareholders in a publicly held corporation. This duty of utmost faith and loyalty has been held to mean that there must be equal treatment of all shareholders.

OUTLINE

E. SALE OF MAJORITY OR CONTROLLING INTEREST

1. **General rule:** A shareholder who obtains a premium for selling a majority or controlling portion of a corporation's stock does *not* have to account to minority shareholders for the premium, *unless* the seller knows, or has reason to believe, that the transfer will result in prejudice to the minority shareholders (e.g., the buyer is (i) a competitor who intends to merge the acquired entity into its own, or (ii) a corporate looter). In the latter instance, the "premium" must be shared with *all* of the stockholders.

2. **Purchase of directorships:** A person who acquires a controlling interest in a corporation can arrange for the (i) seriatim resignations of the present directors, and (ii) appointment of directors who would ordinarily be electable by him. However, in the absence of the sale of a majority or controlling interest in the stock of the corporation, the purchase of directorships is invalid.

IX. FUNDAMENTAL CORPORATE CHANGES

A. SALE OR TRANSFER OF ASSETS

1. **Description:** Where a corporation sells all or substantially all of its assets, the transaction must be approved by the board of directors and a majority (and in some jurisdictions, as provided in the Articles of Incorporation, even a higher proportion) of the shareholders.

   a. A sale of substantially all of the assets occurs when, as a consequence of the transaction, the corporation *cannot* carry on its business activities as presently constituted (i.e., it is *not* necessary for the sale to encompass a specified proportion of corporate assets).

   b. The term "sale" includes voluntarily encumbering substantially all of the corporation's assets.

2. **Exceptions to necessity for shareholder approval:** The board of directors is *not* required to obtain shareholder approval for a sale of all, or substantially all, of a corporation's assets where:

   a. The sale occurs in the ordinary course of business,

   b. Inventory is sold at one location for the purpose of facilitating transfer of the business to other premises,

   c. The corporation was organized for the purpose of transacting the sale (or sales) in question, and

   d. In some jurisdictions, where the corporation is in financial distress.

CORPORATIONS

3. **Appraisal rights of dissenting shareholders:** Where the sale is not for cash or adequately secured promissory notes, some jurisdictions have enacted statutes permitting dissenting shareholders of the corporation which is transferring its assets to receive the cash equivalent of their shares as of the date immediately preceding approval of the sale. To assert this right, a shareholder must ordinarily:

   a. File a written objection to the sale prior to the shareholders' meeting to consider this action,

   b. Vote against the sale,

   c. Give prompt written notice of his desire to assert the appraisal remedy, and

   d. Surrender his shares to the corporation.

4. **Rights of the corporation's creditors**

   a. **Corporate liability:** The corporation disposing of its assets is liable to its creditors for any outstanding obligations. Usually, adequate provision must be made for all creditors from the proceeds of the sale. If the sale is fraudulent, a creditor of the corporation can levy upon the assets which were sold and a constructive trust can be imposed on the consideration received by the corporation.

   b. **Liability of the transferee:** While a transferee is ordinarily not liable to the transferor-corporation's creditors, exceptions to this rule exist where:

      i. The transferor failed to comply with the bulk sales law (in which event, the assets sold may still be levied upon by creditors of the transferring corporation),

      ii. The transfer is a fraudulent conveyance (i.e., was made (i) to defraud the transferor's creditors, or (ii) for less than fair value and resulted in the transferor-corporation becoming insolvent), or

      iii. The transferee assumed the transferor's liabilities.

B. **CORPORATE COMBINATIONS**

1. **Description:** The goal of all corporate combinations is to put the assets of two or more corporations under the control of one management.

2. **Combination types**

   a. **Merger and consolidation:** Five variations:

      i. **Statutory merger:** A merger occurs where one corporation (the "target") is acquired by another corporation (the "surviving corporation"), such that the target is absorbed into the surviving corporation, with the shareholders of the target receiving cash or stock in the surviving corporation in exchange for their target shares. The board of directors of the target distributes this cash or stock to their shareholders, who in turn deliver their shares to the board for cancellation. When the merger is completed, the target ceases to exist and the surviving corporation succeeds to all the rights, liabilities, and assets of the disappearing corporation. Dissenting shareholders of **both** corporations usually have appraisal rights.

(a) **Necessary steps:** To effectuate a merger:

(1) The plan of merger must be approved by the board of directors of **both** corporations.

(2) The plan of merger must be approved by a majority (or, in many jurisdictions, or as provided in the Articles of Incorporation, a higher proportion) of the shareholders of each corporation. In some states, if the corporation has more than one class of voting shares outstanding, a majority of each class voting separately is required to approve the merger.

(3) The plan of merger must be approved by the Secretary of State.

(b) **Short-form merger:** Where a parent corporation owns 90 percent or more of a subsidiary, many jurisdictions allow the subsidiary to merge into the parent without the approval of the shareholders of either corporation. The shareholders of the subsidiary are protected, however, through appraisal rights and by the fiduciary obligations of majority shareholders in freeze-out mergers.

ii. **De facto merger doctrine**

(a) **Description:** In a few jurisdictions, the sale of all a corporation's assets to another corporation is treated as functionally, or "de facto," a statutory merger, entitling the shareholders of both corporations all of the protections (e.g., approval and appraisal rights) shareholders have in statutory mergers. Unless the requisites for a merger have been satisfied, the entire transaction can be rescinded by a creditor or dissenting shareholder. Another consequence of the "de facto merger doctrine" is that the surviving corporation is liable for obligations of the target company, even though there was no express or implied assumption of these debts. The de facto merger doctrine, where applied, is particularly significant for shareholders of the acquiring company, because asset acquisitions do not normally require the approval of the shareholders of the acquiring company, nor are appraisal rights available to them. However, most states have by statute rejected the de facto merger doctrine, and allow corporations to structure transactions as they see fit. Thus an asset purchase will not be subject to the approval of the shareholders of the acquiring corporation unless provision has been made for such approval in the articles of incorporation, or, in some states, if the corporation is issuing stock to purchase the assets having voting power equal to 20 percent or more of the corporation's voting shares prior to the transaction.

    iii. **Triangular merger:** In a triangular merger, the acquiring corporation creates a subsidiary, capitalizing it with cash or shares of its stock. In return, the acquiring corporation gets all of the subsidiary's stock. This wholly owned subsidiary is then merged with the target corporation, with the target shareholders receiving as consideration the assets the acquiring corporation invested in the subsidiary (i.e., cash or shares of the acquiring corporation's stock) in exchange for their shares in the target. If the target is the surviving corporation after the merger, the transaction is a "reverse triangular merger"; if the subsidiary survives, it is a "forward triangular merger." The reverse triangular form is more common because it allows for the continued corporate existence of the target, but now as a wholly owned subsidiary of the acquiring corporation (continued corporate existence of the target may be important for continuing contract rights or licenses held by the target). Advantages of the triangular merger include: (1) the liability of the acquirer limited, as it is shielded by the subsidiary; and (2) approval from the acquirer's shareholders is not needed, since it is the shareholders of the subsidiary that must approve the merger (since the subsidiary is wholly owned by the parent, there is no problem getting the approval), unless approval is required either by statute (e.g., if shares equal to 20 percent or more of the acquiring corporation's voting power prior to the merger are being issued to the target shareholders) or under the acquirer's Articles of Incorporation.

    iv. **Compulsory share exchange:** Some states allow "compulsory share exchanges," a more direct way of accomplishing the same result as a triangular merger. Under a compulsory share exchange, if the target board approves the exchange of shares, and a majority of the target's shareholders approve it, the target shareholders receive the consideration offered by the acquiring corporation (either cash or shares of stock in the acquiring corporation) in exchange for their shares in the target. As they would in a merger, the target shareholders in a compulsory share exchange have appraisal rights.

    v. **Consolidation:** In a consolidation, two or more corporations combine into a new corporation. The constituent corporations cease to exist, a new legal entity is created, and the shareholders exchange their stock for shares in the new entity.

  b. **Exchange of shares (stock swap):** The acquiring corporation issues new shares to shareholders of the target in exchange for their stock in the target. The target then becomes a subsidiary. If not all of the target's shareholders go along, however, the acquirer will be left to deal with minority shareholders in the subsidiary.

    c. **Purchase of assets:** The acquiring corporation buys the assets of the target for stock (or some combination of stock, cash, and/or other securities). The acquiring corporation obtains control over the target's assets, and the target becomes a shell or holding company whose assets consist of the stock, cash, or other securities. Advantages of this technique include:

        i. The target's shareholders do not get appraisal rights (unless the de facto merger doctrine applies in that jurisdiction).

        ii. There are no procedural impediments to the acquirer's management, as shareholder approval is not needed (unless approval is required either by statute, because of the amount of stock being issued in the transaction, or under the acquirer's Articles of Incorporation). A merger or consolidation might require shareholder approval.

Generally, approval by a majority of the outstanding shares is required for sale of "all or substantially all" of the corporation's assets. Shareholder approval is not needed in the case of sales of all or substantially all assets "in the usual and regular course of business." However, such sales are by nature almost never in the usual or regular course of business.

3. **Appraisal rights**

    a. **General rule:** Ordinarily dissenting shareholders of both the target and surviving corporation have appraisal rights in a merger situation.

    b. **Exceptions:** In many jurisdictions, appraisal rights do not exist where the dissenting shareholder's corporation (i) is listed on a national securities exchange, or (ii) has 2,000 or more shareholders. Notwithstanding the foregoing, in most jurisdictions, minority shareholders in short-form mergers are automatically granted appraisal rights.

    c. **Effect of appraisal rights:** Unless a dissenting shareholder can show fraud (as opposed to simply alleged unfairness), appraisal rights often constitute the *exclusive* state law remedy. However, a dissenting shareholder is always entitled to commence an action for violation of *federal* securities laws.

4. **Rights of creditors of the target corporation:** The obligations of the transferor corporation are ordinarily assumed by the survivor.

5. **Acquisition or purchase of shares:** There is ordinarily no requirement that a corporation desiring to acquire another entity by purchasing the stock directly from the latter's shareholders, either on the open market or by tender offer (as described below), obtain the approval of its (or the target's) shareholders or the board of directors of the target.

CORPORATIONS

X. SECURITIES FRAUD AND INSIDER TRADING

A. **"SPECIAL FACTS" DOCTRINE:** Where, as a consequence of one's corporate position, one obtains information about material facts affecting the value of the stock, there is a fiduciary duty to disclose those facts *to an existing shareholder* in connection with a sale or purchase of the corporation's stock.

1. **Damages:** The aggrieved party can recover all damages resulting from the defendant's fraudulent conduct.

2. **Corporate action:** In some jurisdictions, a corporation can maintain this action against an insider if the aggrieved buyer or seller fails to pursue it.

3. **Direct dealing:** In a few states, the "insiders" must have dealt *directly* with the aggrieved party (i.e., there is no liability for over-the-counter sales or purchases via a national stock exchange).

B. **SEC RULE 10b-5:** Under SEC Rule 10b-5, it is unlawful for an insider to use any fraudulent or manipulative means in connection with the sale or purchase of securities by means of an instrumentality of interstate commerce.

1. **Unlawful:** The SEC can recover civil penalties for unlawful trading (to make the culpable party disgorge any profits), plus treble damages. Additionally, *criminal penalties* for insider trading are available and extremely costly.

2. **Securities:** The stock of any public or private corporation is covered by this regulation, as well any corporate indebtedness (such as bonds or debentures).

3. **"Sale or purchase requirement":** Virtually any *transfer of a security* (including its initial issuance) is covered by Rule 10b-5.

    a. Any "contract to sell" or other disposition is covered.

    b. The delivery of stock to promoters for their initial contributions of capital to the corporation is covered.

    c. Stock transferred in the context of a merger or reorganization is also covered.

4. **Instrumentality of interstate commerce:** Use of the mails, the telephone or a telegraph system, at any point in the transaction, is sufficient to satisfy this element (even if only a single intrastate telephone call is made).

5. **"Purchasers or sellers" requirement:** For a private party (a person or entity other than the SEC) to commence an action under Rule 10b-5, the plaintiff must have purchased, sold, issued or received securities. Where a party refrains from taking action on the basis of information which was improperly obtained or disclosed, *no* "purchaser or seller" exists.

6. **Insiders:** One is an "insider" for purposes of Rule 10b-5, where he (1) learns of material, nonpublic information as a consequence of his corporate position, or (2) had a fiduciary relationship to the corporation or the plaintiff. Additionally, tippers are liable for use of their information by tippees when their purpose in transmitting the information is to realize, directly or indirectly, some type of personal benefit or gain. A tippee is liable only if (1) the tipper has liability for the disclosure, and (2) the tippee is, or should have been, aware that the information should not have been disclosed to him.

7. **Fraudulent or manipulative means:** There must be some element of scienter (intent to deceive or take unfair advantage of another) by the defendant.

    a. **Duty of disclosure:** Under Rule 10b-5, an insider is under a duty to disclose *material, nonpublic information* pertaining to the securities being transferred.

    b. **False statements:** Rule 10b-5 is violated when an insider deliberately or recklessly makes a material misrepresentation pertaining to the securities being transferred.

    c. **Negligent statements:** Negligently made misstatements are ***not*** actionable.

8. **Materiality:** A misrepresentation or failure to disclose must pertain to material information (i.e., the type to which a reasonable person would attach significance). In determining if an opinion as to the occurrence of some *prospective* event is material, a court will balance the (1) probability of the event, and (2) anticipated magnitude of that occurrence in light of the totality of the company's activities.

9. **Reliance:** Where the defendant has made a material misrepresentation, the plaintiff must affirmatively prove reliance upon it. However, where there has been a failure to disclose material facts, reliance by the plaintiff is ordinarily presumed.

10. **Civil remedies:** The aggrieved party may:

    a. Rescind the transaction,

    b. Recover the damages which he incurred as a result of the transaction (a reasonable period of time is ordinarily awaited to determine the value of the shares in light of the nondisclosed information), or

    c. Obtain injunctive relief (i.e., cause the defendant to disgorge any losses avoided by the transaction).

    Punitive damages are **not** available under Rule 10b-5.

C. **SECTION 16(b):** Under Section 16(b) of the Exchange Act, a director, officer, or 10 percent shareholder of a corporation which (1) is traded on a national exchange, or (2) has a net worth of at least $5 million and 500 shareholders, is

CORPORATIONS

strictly liable *to that entity* for any *profits* derived from a (1) sale and purchase, or (2) purchase and sale, of the securities of his corporation, within any period of less than six months (the so-called "short-swing profits" rule).

1. **Securities involved:** Unlike under Rule 10b-5, Section 16(b) liability has been limited to equity securities (rather than evidences of indebtedness).

2. **Director, officer, or 10 percent shareholder**

   a. **Director:** A director is (i) anyone who has been authorized to have that title, or (ii) an entity which has appointed or "deputized" another to serve as a director for it. A director need only occupy his *office* at the time of *either* the purchase or sale.

   b. **Officer:** The term "officer" includes persons upon whom the corporation has bestowed such title (president, vice-president, secretary, treasurer, controller) **and** who performs the functions normally associated with that office. (A mere title based only upon sales does *not* suffice.) An officer need only occupy his position at the time of *either* the purchase or sale.

   c. **Ten percent shareholder:** A person is regarded as the beneficial owner of securities held in another's name if, in any manner, he (1) controls the disposition of those shares, or (2) in the view of some courts, derives a financial benefit from those shares which is basically equivalent to ownership. Ten percent shareholders must own that percentage of shares at *both* the time of (1) purchase, *and* (2) sale.

3. **Within any period of less than six months:** The six-month period is six calendar months, excluding the last date which is identical to the original date (i.e., April 5 through September 4, but not September 5). The amounts recoverable under Section 16(b) are computed in a manner which maximizes the profits recoverable. The lowest purchase and highest sale within the six-month period are "matched," then the second lowest purchase and sale are matched, and so forth. No losses during the applicable period may be offset against the profits calculated in the foregoing manner.

   Thus, Section 16(b) is not activated until a shareholder already owns 10 percent of the corporation's shares, and is not applicable after the shareholder ceases to own 10 percent of the corporation's shares.

4. **Purchase and sale, or sale and purchase, requirement:** Whether a transfer of securities which is not a straight forward "purchase" and "sale" is within the purview of Section 16(b) depends upon whether the transaction had a potential for securities abuse (i.e., where receipt of stock was the result of a merger over which the shareholder had no control, the share exchange resulting from the merger did *not* constitute a sale). In addition, SEC rules allow executives to acquire and sell

shares under "tax conditioned" plans without reporting those transactions or facing short-swing profits liability for them. Such plans are either qualified under the Internal Revenue Code or meet the requirements of a qualified stock purchase plan. Thus executives can participate in employee stock purchase plans, for example, and receive distributions on death, disability, retirement, or termination without violating Rule 16(b).

5. **Corporate recovery:** Only the insider's corporation can recover under Section 16(b). If the board of directors fails to initiate an action when there is a likelihood of substantial recovery, a derivative action may be commenced by a shareholder of that entity, whether or not he owned the corporation's shares at the time of the transaction under scrutiny. Additionally, there is no requirement that the shareholder commencing the derivative action post a bond as security for the expenses which are likely to be incurred in defending the action. Because any recovery under a Rule 16(b) derivative action goes to the corporation, and not the shareholder bringing the action, the main reason such actions are brought is that attorneys' fees of a shareholder plaintiff succeeding in a Rule 16(b) derivative action are recoverable from the corporation.

XI. TENDER OFFERS AND TAKEOVER DEFENSES

A. **DEFINITION OF TENDER OFFER: A tender offer is an offer (of cash or securities) to the shareholders of a corporation in exchange for their shares at a premium over the market price.**

 1. **Shareholder approval:** No shareholder vote is required as, strictly speaking, a tender offer is not a corporate transaction from the target's perspective, but the transaction of individual shareholders.

 2. **Board approval:** No board approval is required. There are, however, friendly and hostile offers. A friendly tender offer is one that has the support of the target's board, whereas a hostile offer does not.

B. **FEDERAL REGULATION OF TENDER OFFERS: The Williams Act, passed in 1968, amending the Securities Exchange Act of 1934, was implemented to protect investors and to give the market an early warning of an impending tender offer. The act has the following elements, all relating to the provision of information:**

 1. **No secret purchases:** A party that "directly or indirectly" acquires more than five percent ownership must disclose, within ten days of passing the five percent threshold, certain information such as the party's identity and number of shares held, the source and amount of funds for making share purchases, any arrangements the party has with others concerning shares of the target, and the party's

purposes in acquiring the shares and his intentions regarding the target. Note that the act allows the buyer to continue making purchases during the ten-day period.

2. **Tender offer disclosure:** A bidder must disclose, on the day it commences its tender offer, the information included in the section above, plus additional information, including the purpose of the tender offer, the bidder's plans for the target, past negotiations between the bidder and the target, the bidder's financial statements (if material), regulatory approvals that may be necessary, and any other material information.

3. **Timing**

    a. **Minimum offer period:** The SEC requires tender offers to be kept open for at least 20 business days. If the offeror increases the price, it must keep the offer open for at least 10 days after the announcement of the increase.

    b. **Withdrawal provision:** Anyone who has tendered his shares before the end of the offer period may withdraw his tendered shares within the first 15 days of the tender offer or 10 days following the commencement of a competing bid.

    c. **Policy considerations:** The time provisions give managers the opportunity to react and time to craft defensive tactics. Whether this is good or bad depends on whether one favors defensive tactics. The provisions also facilitate competing bids by creating an auction system. If there are no competing bids, then the offeror is paying a high premium. The shareholders thereby earn higher premiums, and society benefits because control will go to the party that values control the most (instead of the first in line).

4. **Equal treatment:** The buyer must (i) make the same price offer to everyone, and (ii) take the shares *pro rata* if there are too many sellers. Furthermore, during the offer period, shares can only be bought through the offer.

5. **Antifraud provision:** Section 14(e) of the Exchange Act prohibits any false or misleading statements or omissions, as well as any fraudulent, deceptive, or manipulative act, in connection with any tender offer.

    a. **Culpability:** Most courts have held that some culpability (either knowledge of the falsity or reckless disregard for the truth) is required.

        i. **Materiality:** Most courts have held that an omitted fact is material if there is a substantial likelihood that, under all the circumstances, the omitted fact would have assumed actual significance in the shareholder's deliberations.

        ii. **Reliance:** The shareholder must have relied upon the misrepresentation or omission. In cases of omission, where reliance is difficult to prove, reliance is often presumed. Note, however, that a material omission will not support an action under Section 14(e) when the offer is voluntarily withdrawn, because then reliance is impossible.

  iii. **Remedies**

   (a) **Damages:** For damages, the plaintiff must have standing and injury. The target corporation and the tendering and nontendering shareholders may sue for damages. However, the offeror lacks standing to assert damages, since he is not within the class of intended beneficiaries of the Williams Act. The plaintiff must prove injury caused directly by the defendant or through reliance on the defendant's misrepresentations or omissions.

   (b) **Injunction:** To obtain injunctive relief, the plaintiff must show a substantial probability that a violation has occurred or that an irreparable injury will occur.

C. **STATE ANTITAKEOVER STATUTES: States have been more willing to regulate takeovers than the federal government.**

 1. **First-generation statutes:** These statutes regulated the tender offer process itself, imposing greater requirements than the Williams Act. The Supreme Court struck them down, viewing them as hindering interstate commerce.

 2. **Second-generation statutes:** These statutes leave the process alone but regulate those things that fall within the mainstream of state corporate law, for example, voting rights and fiduciary duties. At the formal level, such statutes do not affect the tender offer process, but in practice they do have an impact.

  a. **Control share acquisition statutes:** If an acquiring shareholder crosses a specified threshold, the shares will not have voting rights unless a majority of disinterested shareholders approves those shares for voting rights.

  b. **Fair-price statutes:** Directed against two-tiered takeovers, these statutes impose a supermajority voting requirement for mergers and similar combinations. The voting requirement can be waived, however, if the transaction ensures that those shareholders who did not tender will receive a price at least equal to the highest price the acquirer paid for any of the target's shares over a certain period of time.

  c. **Redemption rights:** If a bidder gains control, minority shareholders have the right to redeem their shares at the value at which the bidder bought the shares.

  d. **Moratorium statutes:** These statutes prohibit any combinations (merger, liquidation, sale of substantially all assets) for a certain period of time after a shareholder has crossed a specified ownership threshold without approval from the board in advance.

CORPORATIONS

D. **TAKEOVER DEFENSES:** A board facing a hostile tender offer, or concerned about the possibility of one, may implement a number of defensive measures designed to thwart the tender offer. These measures can be classified in several ways:

1. **Independence:** These tactics are designed either to keep the corporation independent or to facilitate a favored-partner acquisition (see examples below).

2. **Pre/post-offer**

    a. **Pre-offer (prophylactic or "shark repellent") measures:** Examples of pre-offer measures include: a charter amendment requiring a supermajority vote in order to effect a merger or sale of all assets, a charter amendment creating a class of stockholders with veto power over a merger, an amendment creating a staggered board of directors, accelerated loans in the event of a merger (which does not require charter amendment), and "golden parachutes" for top managers.

    b. **Post-offer measures:** Examples of post-offer measures include: defensive suits, defensive acquisitions, defensive mergers, lockups, share manipulations (such as the poison pill), and a turnabout or Pac-Man defense.

3. **Tactics requiring/not requiring shareholder approval:** Some of the most potent defensive tactics (e.g., poison pills, greenmail, lockup) do not need shareholder approval, thus enabling management to use its powers alone to block a merger. Use of such tactics, however, may raise fiduciary duty concerns.

4. **Definition of selected defensive tactics**

    a. **Poison pill:** One of the most popular defensive tactics, the poison pill has little economic effect absent the triggering event (usually the acquisition, without board consent, of a specified percentage of the corporation's stock), but it can have very substantial effects once triggered. Poison pills may be redeemable or nonredeemable.

        i. **Variations**

            (a) **Rights plan:** The target's common shareholders receive, as a dividend on their shares, rights or warrants which entitle the shareholders (except the bidder) to purchase the target's stock (or stock in the acquiring company if the target does not survive) for a specified period and presumably at a low price. To exercise the rights, of course, there must be a triggering event.

            (b) **Conversion rights:** The target board creates a preferred class of stock which becomes convertible into voting stock of the acquirer ***at a discount***. The charter provisions creating the preferred class would specify that the corporation could not consummate certain transactions unless the acquirer agreed to comply with the provisions of the preferred class.

(c) **Redemption rights:** The target board issues preferred stock whose poisonous aspect is in the stock's redemption rights. Upon a designated triggering event, the holder of the preferred stock can redeem it for a certain value. Note that managers may get away with setting this value arbitrarily high.

b. **Greenmail:** Greenmail refers to the repurchase by the target corporation of a potential bidder's stock, usually at a substantial premium, with the understanding that the bidder will stop the takeover attempt.

　i. **Impact on shareholders:** Greenmail severely affects shareholders' interests, because not only do they lose a chance to sell at a premium to the bidder, but their shares might lose value as a result of the buyout of the bidder. In essence, it is the shareholders who end up paying the premium.

　ii. **Responses:** For the most part, courts have refused to find that the board's decision to pay greenmail violates its fiduciary duties to shareholders, saying that any such decision must be evaluated according to the business judgment rule.

c. **Restructuring defenses:** The target offers target shareholders cash or securities of greater market value than what the bidder offers. There are two basic types of these defenses:

　i. **Leveraged buyout (LBO):** The target's management, in conjunction with an investment banking firm, forms a new corporation to make a rival tender offer. The target often finances the new tender offer by issuing "junk bonds," which will be paid by selling assets of the target or by increasing its leverage. Courts have sometimes found duty of loyalty violations with respect to such transactions.

　ii. **Recapitalization:** Public shareholders exchange most of their stock for cash (at a premium). Management does not exchange its equity, but rather receives new shares or options in lieu of cash. The public shareholder's equity in the company is then reduced and management gains a greater measure of control over the corporation. Because it is financed through substantial borrowings, recapitalization often leads to a sale of assets.

　iii. **Lockup:** The target's management sells a favored bidder a major interest in the company (e.g., a valuable asset or an option to buy newly issued shares) without having to get shareholder approval. This gives a great edge to the favored bidder.

　iv. **Self-tender:** The target makes an offer for its own shares. When a company buys its own shares, the company's value goes down, as well as the share price (the law of conservation of money).

CORPORATIONS

5. **The case for defensive tactics**

   a. **Shareholders may make unwise decisions.** Therefore, it is better for both shareholders and society if such decisions are left up to management. Presumably, disinterested directors would have no incentive to make decisions that are disadvantageous to shareholders.

      i. **Distortions:** The pressure to tender caused by collective action problems creates distortions. Therefore, it can be better for one party to make the decision.

         (a) **Counterarguments:** Even if there are distortions, (i) it may not be clear that it is in the shareholders' best interests for managers to decide, due to a potential conflict of interest; (ii) there are other ways of addressing distortions, such as through redemption rights statutes, that do not create a conflict of interest; and (iii) hostile takeover bidders may design takeovers in such a way as to minimize the pressure to tender (e.g., freezing out at the same price as the acquisition price).

      ii. **The shareholders may be uninformed:** The shareholders may be less informed than management, causing them to make unwise decisions.

         (a) Shareholders might not know elements of the real value of the company (such as research and development and long-term plans). Shareholders may thereby be hurt if the takeover is allowed.

         (b) Ex ante, if the shareholders play a part in the decision-making process, directors may become myopic and begin to focus on the short-term rather than the long-term consequences for the corporation.

      iii. **Externalities:** Even if there are no distortions or misinformation, and even if the shareholders are well educated, some takeovers will be inefficient.

         (a) **Counterarguments:** Even if there are externalities, it is not clear that the best remedy is to give managers the power to block. In fact, it is not clear that managers would always use defensive tactics to block takeovers with negative externalities.

6. **The case against defensive tactics**

   a. **Policy arguments**

      i. **Acquisitions are good**

         (a) **Ex post:** When a takeover succeeds, shareholders are usually made richer, and some efficiency gains result (e.g., the bidder can produce synergy or may run the company more efficiently).

(b) **Ex ante:** Takeovers have disciplinary effects on management. Directors must be responsive to shareholder interests, or a takeover may result.

ii. **Therefore, obstructions are bad**

(a) **Ex post:** Good acquisitions will be lost, as managers attempt to block the takeover for personal reasons (rather than for reasons in the shareholders' best interests).

(b) **Ex ante:** Obstruction dilutes the disciplinary effect.

b. **Legal arguments:** Although managerial investment decisions are protected by the business judgment rule, greater judicial scrutiny of managerial decisions in the context of takeovers is justified because:

i. **Potential conflict of interest:** The managers' jobs are at stake if the corporation is taken over.

ii. **Corporate control market:** There is no need to scrutinize managerial decisions very closely in the run-of-the-mill investment decision because there is a place in the market for corporate control, which has a disciplinary effect on managers. Defensive tactics destroy this market.

iii. **Shareholder participation is viable:** It would be inefficient to have shareholders involved in running the company; however, shareholder participation can be necessary when it comes to fundamental changes.

XII. DISSOLUTION AND LIQUIDATION

A. **DEFINITIONS:** When a corporation terminates its corporate business, it liquidates. When it ceases to exist as a legal entity, it dissolves.

1. **How do corporations dissolve?** Corporations may dissolve voluntarily or involuntarily. A voluntary dissolution generally *requires a majority vote of both the board members and the shareholders*. Involuntary dissolution is, in rare circumstances (unless otherwise provided by statute), ordered by a court. Under the common law, such an involuntary dissolution is initiated by a suit by shareholders or directors and may be on the grounds of fraud, dissension, deadlock, gross mismanagement, or abuse of the minority shareholders. Statutes in various jurisdictions provide for a shareholder or director right of petition for dissolution on similar grounds. Even so, a petition for dissolution is rarely granted for publicly held corporations. Finally, the state may petition for the dissolution of a corporation that has abused its authority or that has failed to meet important statutory requirements.

CORPORATIONS

2. **How do corporations liquidate?** Generally, a corporation dissolves and subsequently liquidates. To liquidate, the corporation pays its debts and distributes its assets. Even after dissolution, a corporation remains liable for its debts. It must wind up all corporate business within a reasonable time. If it does not, the directors may become personally liable for the corporation's debts. After a liquidation, the shareholders receive a pro rata share of any assets that remain after all debts and obligations have been paid. The Articles of Incorporation sometimes differentiate between classes of shares (i.e., preferred or common) in terms of their rights to liquidate distributions. A liquidation preference offers one class of shares a priority in the distribution process.

MULTIPLE-CHOICE QUESTION
TOPIC LIST

1. Corporate formation—de jure corporations
2. Doctrine of corporation by estoppel
3. Piercing the corporate veil
4. Piercing the corporate veil
5. Pre-incorporation stock subscription agreements
6. Piercing the corporate veil—undercapitalization
7. Management of the corporation's affairs—sale of corporate assets
8. Powers of the board of directors—charitable donations
9. Powers of the board of directors—by-law amendment
10. Ultra vires doctrine
11. Election of the board of directors
12. Election of the board of directors—cumulative voting
13. Election of the board of directors—straight voting
14. Removal of a director from the board
15. Removal of a director from the board
16. How a board operates—quorum
17. How a board operates—informal actions
18. How a board operates—special meetings of the board
19. How a board operates—notice and quorum
20. Conflicts of interest
21. Voting—Ties
22. Voting—Prospective agreements
23. Appointment of corporate officers
24. Corporate officers—decision-making powers
25. Corporate officers—authority of office
26. Implied authority—custom and practice

CORPORATIONS

27. Apparent authority

28. Inspection of corporate books and records

29. Corporate opportunity doctrine

30. Officer compensation

31. Competition with one's own corporation

32. Solicitation of key personnel

33. Failure to disclose material information

34. SEC Rule 10b-5 liability

35. Remedies under SEC Rule 10b-5

36. Election of the board of directors by majority shareholders

37. Sale of all of a corporation's assets

38. Shareholder approval of the sale of substantially all of a corporation's assets

39. Remedies of shareholders who object to the sale of substantially all of a corporation's assets

40. Shareholder access to books and records of the corporation

MULTIPLE-CHOICE QUESTIONS

Questions 1–2 refer to the following fact pattern:

ExamPrep Co. is located in the state of Utopia and has been in operation for four years. Its corporate purpose is to prepare law students for exams through tutorials, seminars, and distribution of exam preparation materials. ExamPrep Co. is extremely successful thanks to its charismatic instructors, the zeal of its founder, and the thoroughness of its texts. Its enrollment has therefore steadily risen over the years it has been in operation.

The state of Utopia requires that, for a corporation to be properly formed, it must deliver a properly completed set of the Articles of Incorporation to the secretary of state and pay a $250 filing fee. Utopia also directs corporations to place an ad in the newspaper in the town in which the corporation's headquarters are located in order to inform residents of its existence, but this is not a requirement for incorporation.

1. For the purposes of this question only, assume that ExamPrep Co. filed its Articles of Incorporation with the secretary of state and paid the $250 filing fee upon initiating its operations four years ago but did not place the ad in the newspaper. Should ExamPrep Co. be considered a corporation for all purposes?

   (A) Yes, if Utopia is a state that recognizes corporations as de jure if they have substantially complied with all mandatory requirements for corporations.
   (B) No, because ExamPrep Co. is probably a de facto corporation.
   (C) Yes, because ExamPrep Co. paid the required filing fee.
   (D) No, because ExamPrep Co. did not place the ad in the newspaper.

2. For purposes of this question only, assume that ExamPrep Co. has neither filed Articles of Incorporation with the secretary of state nor paid the filing fee. Furthermore, it has never tried to comply with either statutory requirement. It has, however, advertised itself as a corporation and represents itself as such to its students. John, a law student at the University of Utopia, sees ExamPrep Co.'s ads and decides to enroll in one of ExamPrep Co.'s Corporations seminars. Included in the enrollment materials is a certificate stating that ExamPrep Co. will refund the money of any student who does not earn at least a B grade on his final Corporations exam. John attends all sessions of the seminar but only earns a C+ on his final Corporations exam. He takes his exam to the president of ExamPrep Co. and requests a refund. However, the president refuses to refund John's money. Incensed, John sues ExamPrep Co. for the full amount of his tuition. Who will prevail?

   (A) ExamPrep Co., because it is not a corporation and is not required to honor any contracts made.
   (B) ExamPrep Co., because it is a de facto corporation.
   (C) John, because he reasonably believed that he was dealing with a corporation, and ExamPrep Co. must honor its contract with him.
   (D) John, because he did not earn a B on his final exam.

CORPORATIONS

Questions 3–4 refer to the following fact pattern:

Darlene Dogwalker forms a corporation called Dogwalkers. In doing so, she meets all statutory requirements and directives for corporate formation. The corporation's business is dog walking and pet care.

Despite its name, which suggests that there is more than one "Dogwalker," Dogwalkers has only one shareholder: Darlene. Darlene asks her brother, Daniel Dogwalker, and her mother, Debbie Catgroomer-Dogwalker, to serve on Dogwalkers' board of directors. Darlene also sets up a bank account for Dogwalkers and deposits all corporate proceeds into that account.

Unfortunately, Darlene's proceeds are few, and she is forced to shut down her business after only a few months. Much to her dismay, Darlene has to move in with her mother because she is personally insolvent.

3. Leashes, Inc. sues Dogwalkers and Darlene in her individual capacity for the money it is owed for leashes Dogwalkers bought. Darlene moves to dismiss the action against her personally. Judgment for whom?

   (A) Darlene, because she is personally insolvent.
   (B) Darlene, as long as Dogwalkers was a separate corporate entity and did not commit fraud or injustice.
   (C) Leashes, Inc., because Darlene was the sole shareholder of Dogwalkers.
   (D) Leashes, Inc., if the board of directors did not meet regularly.

4. For purposes of this question only, assume that Darlene had an agreement with Walking Doggies, her former employer, that she would not work in the dog walking business for three years. Two years after leaving Walking Doggies, Darlene formed Dogwalkers. Walking Doggies sues Darlene and Dogwalkers for an injunction prohibiting Darlene from walking dogs and for damages sustained from Darlene's violation of the noncompetition agreement. Darlene moves to dismiss the suit against her on the grounds that Dogwalkers, not she, is competing with Walking Doggies. Who will prevail?

   (A) Walking Doggies, if Darlene incorporated Dogwalkers in order to evade the noncompetition agreement.
   (B) Walking Doggies, even if Darlene is walking dogs in a state two thousand miles away.
   (C) Darlene, because Dogwalkers, not she, is competing with Walking Doggies.
   (D) Darlene, because she is personally insolvent and is no longer walking dogs.

Questions 5–6 refer to the following fact pattern:

Bill and Ted decide to form a corporation to provide tours around the world. They plan to call their company "Excellent Adventures." Excellent Adventures will provide gourmet meals, five-star lodging, first-class transportation, personal services such as Shiatsu massage and shoe shining, and entertainment to any guests fortunate enough to travel on one of the company's tours.

In order to capitalize their corporation, they decide to issue 100 shares of stock to interested subscribers. Several subscribers, including Mohammed, agree to purchase some shares at Bill and Ted's asking price of $3 per share. Bill and Ted then incorporate Excellent Adventures in the state of Blackacre.

5. For the purposes of this question only, assume that Mohammed wishes to back out of his agreement to purchase shares in Excellent Adventures. He indicates his intent to do so after Excellent Adventures has been properly formed. The other shareholders still wish to proceed with the deal and do not release Mohammed. Excellent Adventures sues to enforce its agreement with Mohammed. Who will prevail?

   (A) Mohammed, if Blackacre has adopted the minority rule on pre-incorporation stock subscriptions.
   (B) Mohammed, because he can revoke his agreement to subscribe at any time.
   (C) Excellent Adventures, because it is a validly formed corporation.
   (D) Excellent Adventures, if Blackacre has adopted the minority rule on pre-incorporation stock subscriptions.

6. For the purposes of this question only, assume that Excellent Adventures must spend $1000 per customer to provide world tours and that Bill and Ted are the sole shareholders of Excellent Adventures. Bill and Ted each own 50 shares and bought them for $3. Excellent Adventures contracts with Globetrotters, a group of American retirees, to tour 40 people around the world. The group leaves Los Angeles, arrives in Beijing, and finds itself with no accommodations, no tour guide, and no Chinese/English dictionary. A retired attorney in the group proposes that the group sue Excellent Adventures and Bill and Ted in their individual capacities. Will Globetrotters prevail against Bill and Ted?

   (A) Yes, because Excellent Adventures did not provide the world tour.
   (B) Yes, because Excellent Adventures was undercapitalized for its corporate purpose.
   (C) No, because Bill and Ted are protected by the corporate shield.
   (D) No, if Bill and Ted did not personally lead the tour.

Questions 7–10 refer to the following fact pattern:

Beautiful Mountain Corp. ("BMC") is a corporation in the state of Mountainland—a northern New England state—whose primary corporate purpose is selling mountain climbing equipment. For 13 years, mountain climbers from all over New England have flocked to BMC to purchase its top-of-the-line equipment. BMC also has a very popular website and mail-order catalog. BMC prides itself on always stocking the very finest and most up-to-date items.

CORPORATIONS

7. For the purposes of this question only, assume that in 1999, BMC's board of directors decides to liquidate all of the corporation's assets and donate the proceeds to the Hare Krishna, a religious group of which the board's chair is a devoted member. The shareholders sue, claiming that this is an inappropriate action for the board to take. Who will prevail?

   (A) The shareholders, if BMC is a closely held corporation.
   (B) The shareholders, because the sale of substantially all of a corporation's assets normally requires shareholder approval.
   (C) The board of directors, because the management of a corporation's affairs is vested in its board of directors.
   (D) The board of directors, because it is not required to answer to the shareholders.

8. For the purposes of this question only, assume that BMC's Articles of Incorporation authorize the board of directors to take all legal action. Climber Rescue, Inc. ("CRI") asks BMC to fund efforts to rescue three climbers who were lost in an avalanche in the Berkshires. The board of directors asks BMC's attorney whether it has the authority to fund this activity. What will the attorney answer?

   (A) No, because rescue efforts are not part of BMC's corporate purpose.
   (B) No, if the Articles of Incorporation do not contemplate rescue efforts.
   (C) Yes, if funding the rescue effort would benefit BMC in the long run.
   (D) Yes, because the management of a corporation's affairs is vested in its board of directors.

9. For the purposes of questions 9 and 10 only, assume that CRI asks BMC to fund the rescue effort but that BMC's Articles of Incorporation do not authorize the directors to take all legal action. BMC's current by-laws state that BMC shall not involve itself in mountain disasters, as it sells climbing equipment and does not want the public to perceive that its equipment contributes to such incidents. In spite of this by-law, BMC's board of directors votes to fund the rescue effort. Is the vote valid?

   (A) Yes, it may be, because the management of a corporation's affairs is vested in its board of directors.
   (B) Yes, it may be, if the directors are empowered to amend the by-laws and their action is considered an implied amendment thereof.
   (C) No, probably not, because the by-laws prohibited such funding.
   (D) No, under the ultra vires doctrine.

10. For the purposes of this question only, assume that the board may only amend the by-laws by passing a formal resolution to do so. Assume also that CRI has no knowledge of the contents of BMC's by-laws. After voting to fund the rescue effort and telling CRI that it will help, the board of directors decides not to fund the effort after all. May CRI sue BMC for the amount it had pledged?

    (A) Yes, in most jurisdictions, because CRI and BMC entered into a contract.
    (B) Yes, in most jurisdictions, because BMC has no ultra vires defense.
    (C) No, unless the rescue effort had not yet begun.
    (D) No, because in most jurisdictions, only a shareholder may sue to enjoin performance of an agreement that is beyond the scope of the corporation's authority.

Questions 11–13 refer to the following fact pattern:

Delectable Dinners, Inc. ("DDI") is a corporation whose primary corporate purpose is preparing dinner for attorneys and other professionals who must work late into the evening. Because lawyers at large firms in Dodge City (where DDI is headquartered) must typically bill at least 2,500 hours per year, DDI delivers a lot of dinners! In addition to the typical pizza and Chinese food selections offered by other delivery services, DDI's menus include sushi, vegetarian entrees, Cambodian food, fried chicken, heavenly desserts, and many other treats. DDI also operates until 2:00 a.m. and guarantees food delivery within 30 minutes. DDI is therefore the food delivery service of choice in Dodge City. DDI has a seven-member board of directors.

11. For the purposes of this question only, assume that Jeanette James, a member of DDI's board of directors, is first elected to the board for a two-year term beginning in February of 1999. However, in December of 1999, she moves to another state for personal reasons and decides to resign because travelling to board meetings would be an onerous responsibility. What should DDI do to replace Ms. James on the board?

   (A) Call a special meeting of the shareholders and have them vote in a new director for a full two-year term of office.
   (B) The president of the board should select someone to replace Ms. James.
   (C) Call a special meeting of the shareholders and have them vote in a new director for the months remaining until the next annual meeting, at which time the shareholders should elect a director for a full term of office.
   (D) The majority of the board of directors should elect someone to replace Ms. James for the months remaining until the next annual meeting, at which time the shareholders should elect a director for a full term of office.

12. For the purposes of this question only, assume that DDI's by-laws provide for cumulative voting for directors. Cumulative voting is allowed by the jurisdiction in which DDI is incorporated. Wendy Darling owns 150 shares in DDI. She is very interested in having her friend, Peter Pan, elected as a director. However, her brother, Michael Darling, who owns 350 shares in DDI, opposes Peter and wants Tinkerbelle. The total number of DDI's shares outstanding is 500. If three directors are up for election, can Michael prevent Peter's election?

   (A) No, because he does not own enough of DDI to choose all three members of the board.
   (B) No, because under principles of corporate fairness, Wendy should be able to elect at least one director.
   (C) Yes, because according to the proportion of the share ownership, Wendy can only vote for one director.
   (D) Yes, because he owns enough of DDI to choose all three members of the board.

CORPORATIONS

13. For the purposes of this question only, assume that the jurisdiction where DDI is located does not require cumulative voting for the election of directors and that DDI's by-laws provide for straight voting. As we saw in question 12, Wendy Darling owns 150 shares in DDI. She is very interested in having her friend, Peter Pan, elected as a director. However, her brother, Michael Darling, who owns 350 shares in DDI, opposes Peter and wants Tinkerbelle. The total number of DDI's shares outstanding is 500. Can Michael prevent Peter's election?

    (A) No, because he does not own enough of DDI to choose all three members of the board.
    (B) No, because under principles of corporate fairness, Wendy should be able to elect at least one director.
    (C) Yes, because according to the proportion of the share ownership, Wendy can only vote for one director.
    (D) Yes, because he owns enough of DDI to choose all three members of the board.

Questions 14–15 refer to the following fact pattern:

Julie Andrews' Fans, Inc. ("JAF") is a corporation whose primary corporate purpose is the sale and distribution of Julie Andrews souvenirs, videos, and recordings. All JAF employees are required to know all of the lyrics to *Edelweiss* and ***Supercalifrajolisticexpialidocius***. JAF's board of directors consists of five members.

Maria Von Trapp became a member of JAF's board at the shareholders' election at the annual meeting that was held only four months ago. Maria defrauds the corporation by bootlegging copies of ***The Sound of Music*** and selling them for her personal profit.

14. Can she be immediately removed from the board of directors?

    (A) Yes, by a majority vote of the other directors.
    (B) Yes, by a majority vote of the shareholders.
    (C) No, if her sales of the bootlegged copies benefited the corporation in some way.
    (D) No, because the shareholders must wait until the next annual meeting to vote her out.

15. Can a court intervene to remove Maria from JAF's board?

    (A) Yes, if the shareholders refuse to remove her.
    (B) Yes, because the shareholders must sue to remove Maria from the board.
    (C) No, because the directors have the power to make decisions on behalf of the corporation.
    (D) No, because the shareholders may decide whether or not to remove a director for fraud.

Questions 16–19 refer to the following fact pattern:

Lawyers for the Cure, Inc. ("LCI") is a corporation whose primary corporate purpose is raising research dollars for AIDS. Over the years, LCI has become the leading charity subscribed to by attorneys. In fact, through its Spring Fling, its Holiday Hoedown, and its summer barbecue, LCI has raised many millions of dollars. It has also become a status symbol to be a member of LCI's board, and attorneys all over the state vie for the honor on an annual basis. LCI's board of directors has seven members.

16. At a board meeting, Tom Thompson, president of LCI's board, proposes a resolution that LCI sponsor the AIDS bike-a-thon each year. How many board members must be present at the board meeting to vote on it?

    (A) Only Tom, as he has the authority, as president of the board, to make such decisions on behalf of LCI.
    (B) A majority of the board members, unless the by-laws state otherwise.
    (C) All of the board members, because such decisions ordinarily require unanimity.
    (D) One-third of the board members, because such decisions are minor compared to the rest of corporate business.

17. For the purposes of this question only, assume that Tom wants to get his resolution passed quickly but that there is no upcoming board meeting scheduled. Can he get the resolution through without a board meeting?

    (A) Yes, if the by-laws allow it.
    (B) Yes, if all of the directors approve it in writing.
    (C) Yes, if a majority of the directors approve it in writing.
    (D) No, resolutions may never be passed except in a formal gathering of the board.

18. For the purposes of this question only, assume that Tom wants to get his resolution passed quickly but that there is no upcoming board meeting scheduled. Can Tom call a special board meeting?

    (A) Yes, because the resolution is important.
    (B) Yes, if the by-laws allow it and he gives reasonable notice.
    (C) No, because corporations hold only one board meeting each year.
    (D) No, because a majority of the shareholders must decide that a special meeting is necessary.

19. For the purposes of this question only, assume that LCI's by-laws allow for special meetings to be held with five days notice. Tom gave only three days notice for the special meeting he called. Only three members (including Tom) attended, and they passed the resolution. Is the resolution valid and enforceable?

    (A) Yes, if another director subsequently ratifies and approves the resolution.
    (B) Yes, because the defect in notice was immaterial.
    (C) No, because there was not a quorum at the meeting.
    (D) No, because Tom did not give adequate notice.

CORPORATIONS

Questions 20–22 refer to the following fact pattern:

Totally Terrific Tours ("TTT"), a corporation that takes people on tours of the American Southwest, has seven members on its board of directors. Although TTT's tours are totally terrific, TTT has had some troubles over the years because the food it has served has not been very tasty. In addition, some clients have reported feeling quite ill after eating TTT's Tex-Mex and barbecue offerings. When word of TTT's nasty cuisine began to spread, TTT's subscriptions noticeably dropped. TTT's board recognizes the need to improve TTT's food service and therefore votes on a resolution to enter into a joint venture with Best Burritos—the very best burritos in the Southwest—so that TTT may serve them to its clients.

20. For the purposes of this question only, assume that Tanya, a member of TTT's board, is the majority shareholder of Best Burritos. Should Tanya vote on the resolution?

    (A) Yes, if she can be objective.
    (B) Yes, because Best Burritos are the best burritos in the Southwest, and TTT needs to offer some decent food.
    (C) No, unless she will vote against the resolution.
    (D) No, because she has a conflict of interest.

21. For the purposes of this question only, assume that Tanya does not vote on the resolution. The other six directors vote. Three vote for the resolution, and three vote against it. What is the proper procedure for the board to decide the resolution?

    (A) The board should consider that the resolution passed, because in the case of a tie the presumption is that a resolution will pass.
    (B) If the by-laws allow it, the directors should vote again and again until they break the tie.
    (C) The board should consider that the resolution failed, because in the case of a tie the presumption is that a resolution will fail.
    (D) If the by-laws allow it, a provisional director may be judicially appointed to decide the issue.

22. For the purposes of this question only, assume that, before the vote occurs, four of the directors agree among themselves to vote for the resolution. When the actual vote occurs, however, only three of them vote for it. The resolution therefore fails. May the shareholders sue to enforce the agreement?

    (A) No, because prospective agreements among directors to vote a certain way are ordinarily void.
    (B) No, because votes of the board are final except in exceptional circumstances.
    (C) Yes, because prospective agreements among directors to vote a certain way are ordinarily valid.
    (D) Yes, because the shareholders have the power to make this kind of decision for the corporation.

Questions 23–27 refer to the following fact pattern:

Legal Grounds is a coffee company in the state of Springfield. It has 19 stores in the state and employs out-of-work attorneys who serve coffee while offering legal advice. Legal Grounds provides malpractice insurance for the attorneys who work there, and local law firms know that, by going to Legal Grounds, they can kill two birds with one stone: get some great coffee and find theretofore unnoticed legal talent. Legal Grounds also sells T-shirts, coffee mugs, and leather portfolios embossed with the Legal Grounds logo.

Legal Grounds has five members on its board of directors.

23. For the purposes of this question only, assume that the president of Legal Grounds resigns. How will a new president be appointed?

    (A) The outgoing president will select her successor.
    (B) The shareholders will elect a new president at their next annual meeting.
    (C) The shareholders will elect a new president immediately.
    (D) The board of directors will choose a new president.

24. For the purposes of this question only, assume that the vice-president of Legal Grounds negotiates a deal with Coffee Klatch, Inc., another company, to provide it with coffee for its stores. The president objects, saying that the vice-president has no authority to enter into such an agreement. The vice-president asserts that he does have such power. Who is correct?

    (A) The president, because she has veto power over any deals that the vice-president makes.
    (B) The president, because she is ultimately responsible for Legal Grounds' bottom line.
    (C) The vice-president, because vice-presidents typically have a separate set of duties from presidents.
    (D) The vice-president, if this is a jurisdiction that allows a vice-president to bind the corporation to transactions that are clearly within the scope of its business.

25. For the purposes of this question only, assume that the Corporate Coffee Grinder, an assistant vice-president, enters into an agreement to purchase, on behalf of the corporation, a very expensive industrial-strength coffee grinder. The corporation wishes to repudiate the agreement. May it do so?

    (A) Yes, because the Corporate Coffee Grinder, as an assistant vice-president, is a minor officer and therefore does not have the authority to make major purchases on behalf of the corporation.
    (B) Yes, because the board of directors must approve major purchases.
    (C) No, because the purchase will not cause the corporation to declare bankruptcy.
    (D) No, because the Corporate Coffee Grinder may purchase equipment reasonably related to coffee grinding.

26. For the purposes of this question only, assume that Legal Grounds uses so much coffee that coffee grinders, even industrial-strength ones, must be replaced at least every six months. The Corporate Coffee Grinder has therefore purchased coffee grinders for Legal Grounds on several previous occasions without objection from the board. However, after reviewing Legal Grounds' expenditures for 1999, the board objects to the Corporate Coffee Grinder's prior purchases. May it object?

    (A) Yes, because the Corporate Coffee Grinder has never asked for approval before buying the coffee grinders.
    (B) Yes, if the Corporate Coffee Grinder is contracting on behalf of the corporation.
    (C) No, because the board has never previously objected.
    (D) No, if the Corporate Coffee Grinder is an attorney.

27. For the purposes of this question only, assume that the Corporate Coffee Grinder, a corporate officer, does not have the authority to contract on behalf of the corporation. However, he contracts with Coffee Grinders, Inc. to provide coffee grinders to Legal Grounds on a biannual basis for the next three years. Legal Grounds seeks to repudiate the agreement on the grounds that the Corporate Coffee Grinder does not have the authority to enter into such contracts. What result?

    (A) Legal Grounds will lose, because the corporation needs coffee grinders and it can only repudiate contracts made for goods or services that it cannot use.
    (B) Legal Grounds will lose, if it should have recognized that Coffee Grinders, Inc. was likely to view the Corporate Coffee Grinder as possessing such authority.
    (C) Legal Grounds will win, because the Corporate Coffee Grinder did not have the authority to enter into such a contract.
    (D) Legal Grounds will win, because the contract is void for lack of consideration.

Questions 28–29 refer to the following fact pattern:

Baby Buggies, Inc. ("BBI") is a corporation whose primary corporate purpose is the manufacture, distribution, and sale of designer baby carriages, prams, and joggers. It also sells printed, quilted covers for the products it carries and fleecy snugglies that fit inside the products to keep babies warm.

BBI's board of directors has seven members. A requirement for membership on the board is practical experience wheeling babies around in strollers of various types. Jocelyn Wang, through her work as a member of BBI's board, learns of a great opportunity to sell pram covers to new mothers in the state of Sleeplessness. She therefore decides to start her own business to make and sell hand-crocheted covers for carriages and prams. She plans to inspect BBI's books and copy its mailing lists to get a customer base. However, BBI learns of Jocelyn's ulterior motive.

28. BBI tells Jocelyn that she may not review the books and records. Jocelyn claims that, as a member of the board, she has an inalienable right to do so. Who is correct?

    (A) Jocelyn, because directors may inspect their corporation's books and records.
    (B) Jocelyn, because her product line will not compete with BBI's main product line.
    (C) BBI, because Jocelyn would be misusing the information.
    (D) BBI, because directors do not have the right to inspect their corporation's books and records.

29. BBI tells Jocelyn that she may not exploit the information she received about the marketing opportunity in Sleeplessness. Jocelyn disagrees, saying that it is a free country where capitalism flourishes. Who is right?

    (A) BBI, because the corporate opportunity doctrine applies in this case.
    (B) BBI, if it was previously marketing covers in Sleeplessness.
    (C) Jocelyn, because it is a free country where capitalism flourishes.
    (D) Jocelyn, because BBI did not learn of the opportunity first.

Questions 30–32 refer to the following fact pattern:

Fabulous Fish Co. ("FFC") is a chain of seafood restaurants in the state of Utopia. It is run by a seven-member board of directors. FFC restaurants are known for their theme restaurants, which feature large lobster tanks, crazy fish wallpaper, and waiters wearing fish hats. FFC is also known for its delicious, award-winning fish chowder.

30. For the purposes of this question only, assume that Henry Halibut is paid $1,000,000/year for his position as the guardian of the top-secret fish chowder recipe. May the shareholders challenge this use of corporate funds?

    (A) No, because the board of directors has total discretion as to what to pay its officers.
    (B) No, if Henry negotiated this salary as a part of his contract.
    (C) Yes, if his salary is unreasonable.
    (D) Yes, if he has only worked at FFC for one year.

31. For the purposes of questions 31 and 32 only, assume that Felicia Fish is a member of FFC's board of directors. Felicia is also an amateur cook. She enjoys experimenting with recipes and loves to surprise her friends and family with delicious new treats. Felicia's husband, Frank, is a fish-lover. One cold night, Felicia surprises him with her very own fish chowder. When he tastes it, he says, "Honey, this is the best fish chowder I've ever eaten. I think it's even better than FFC's fish chowder. You should start your own business selling this stuff!" May Felicia do so while remaining on FFC's board?

    (A) Yes, because directors are not automatically disqualified from being engaged in a business that is in competition with that of their corporation.
    (B) Yes, although she should keep her fish chowder business a secret.
    (C) No, because FFC has won a lot of awards for its fish chowder.
    (D) No, because directors are automatically disqualified from being engaged in a business that is in competition with that of their corporation.

CORPORATIONS

32. Felicia does not know anything about marketing—she's a chef! She decides to ask her friend, Larry Lobster, FFC's marketing director, to come aboard her new enterprise as vice-president in charge of marketing. May she recruit him?

    (A) No, not at any point in time.
    (B) No, at least not until she resigns from FFC's board.
    (C) Yes, because Larry Lobster is a free agent.
    (D) Yes, because under the 13th Amendment, FFC cannot force Larry to keep working there.

Questions 33–35 refer to the following fact pattern:

The Three Little Pigs are directors of BuildAHouse Co., a corporation in the state of Fairyland. BuildAHouse Co. provides home design services, building, and weatherproofing for existing homes. BuildAHouse Co. guarantees that the homes it builds or weatherproofs will withstand all natural and animal disasters. For the 20 years that BuildAHouse Co. has been in existence, no home it has built and/or weatherproofed has ever blown down. Its stock, which is publicly traded, is therefore very valuable.

However, in the spring of 1999, the Three Little Pigs begin to get letters from customers in Fairyland demanding refunds. These customers claim that their BuildAHouse homes have been blown down by the Big Bad Wolf. They further claim that this destruction falls within the animal disaster clause of BuildAHouse's guarantee.

The Three Little Pigs put their heads together to decide what to do about this customer relations crisis. They decide that they should hide the fact that the Big Bad Wolf is blowing down BuildAHouse houses because the end of the quarter is approaching and they do not want shareholders to get concerned. They therefore issue their quarterly report with no mention of the Big Bad Wolf problem.

After reading the quarterly report, the Three Bears, who own shares in BuildAHouse Co., decide to keep their shares instead of selling them. They then learn about the Big Bad Wolf problem.

33. Which of the following may the Three Bears do?

    (A) The Three Bears may file a complaint with the Three Little Pigs.
    (B) The Three Bears may sue the Three Little Pigs.
    (C) The Three Bears may file a complaint with the Securities and Exchange Commission.
    (D) All of the above.

34. Are the Three Little Pigs liable to the Three Bears under SEC Rule 10b-5?

    (A) No, because the information about the Big Bad Wolf was immaterial.
    (B) No, because there was no purchase or sale of securities.
    (C) Yes, because their omission was not fraudulent.
    (D) Yes, because the shareholders should have been provided with the information.

35. For the purposes of this question only, assume that the Three Bears, in reliance upon the quarterly report, decided to buy additional shares. If they may sue the corporation under Rule 10b-5, which of the following is NOT an available remedy?

    (A) Rescission of the transaction.
    (B) Recovery of the damages they suffered from the transaction.
    (C) Injunctive relief whereby the corporation must disgorge any losses avoided by the transaction.
    (D) Punitive damages.

MULTIPLE-CHOICE QUESTIONS

Questions 36–40 refer to the following fact pattern:

Happy Holiday Corp. ("HHC") is a corporation in the state of Vacationland. Its primary corporate purpose is selling vacation properties (e.g., condos, time shares) in Vacationland. Vacationland is a popular vacation destination for couples, families, and college students. It is a prime location because it has beautiful beaches on the coast and rugged mountains inland. Visitors can ski in the winter and surf in the summer. For this reason, HHC is extremely successful.

HHC has a seven-member board of directors and numerous shareholders. Horatio Holiday, HHC's founder, owns the majority of HHC's shares. The remainder of the shares are divided among officers and directors and shareholders who have bought shares through a national stock exchange.

36. Assume for the purposes of this question only that Horatio Holiday demands the resignation of the current directors and makes plans unilaterally to appoint new ones. The other shareholders protest vehemently, saying that they have the right to elect the directors. Horatio smugly tells them that they are full of hot air. Who is correct?

    (A) The other shareholders, because they have the right to elect the directors.
    (B) The other shareholders, because otherwise Horatio would run the company.
    (C) Horatio, because he owns a controlling interest in the company.
    (D) None of the above.

37. Assume for the purposes of this question only that the economy takes a sudden turn for the worse and people are no longer flocking to Vacationland. Stuck with 100 condos that it cannot sell, HHC decides to sell off all of its corporate assets at rock-bottom prices to another real estate developer. HHC is therefore no longer able to carry on its present business activities. If Vacationland follows the majority rule, who must approve the transaction?

    (A) The board of directors and Horatio Holiday.
    (B) Horatio Holiday only.
    (C) All of the shareholders.
    (D) HHC's directors and officers.

38. Assume for the purposes of this question only that the economy does not tank but that HHC's board of directors decides to increase its development of condos and vacation homes through Siestaland Vacations, Inc. ("SVI"), a wholly-owned subsidiary of HHC located in Siestaland. Siestaland is a very restful up-and-coming vacation destination on the other side of the United States from Vacationland. HHC's board decides to sell substantially all of HHC's assets in Vacationland and to transfer these assets to SVI. If Vacationland follows the majority rule, who must approve this transaction?

    (A) The board of directors and Horatio Holiday.
    (B) The board of directors only.
    (C) Horatio Holiday only.
    (D) All of the shareholders.

39. Assume for the purposes of this question only that the sale of HHC's assets is not for cash. Assume also that Vacationland is a jurisdiction that allows dissenting shareholders of a corporation that is transferring its assets to receive the cash equivalent of their shares as of the date immediately preceding approval of the sale. Which of the following is NOT required of a shareholder who wants to assert this right?

    (A) Voting against the sale.
    (B) Appearing personally and stating an objection at the shareholders' meeting that will consider the action.
    (C) Giving prompt written notice of her desire to assert the appraisal remedy.
    (D) Surrendering her shares to the corporation.

40. For the purposes of this question only, assume that Horatio does NOT own a controlling interest in the corporation. He and a few of his friends are corrupt, however, and frequently violate their duty of care. A few of the other shareholders decide to mount a proxy contest to get rid of Horatio and three of his director cronies. They prepare a mailing to be sent to the other shareholders. What is the proper mechanism for doing so?

    (A) They must research the names and addresses of the shareholders themselves and then mail the materials to them, incurring the costs personally.
    (B) They must research the names and addresses of the shareholders themselves and mail the mailing, but HHC should reimburse them for the mailing costs.
    (C) They may look in HHC's books for the names and addresses of the shareholders, but they must mail the materials themselves and incur the costs of doing so personally.
    (D) They may look in HHC's books for the names and addresses of the shareholders, and HHC must mail the materials and incur the costs of doing so.

ANSWERS TO MULTIPLE-CHOICE QUESTIONS

1. **(A)** Choice (A) is correct because, if a jurisdiction recognizes corporations that have substantially complied with all requirements, a corporation does not need to comply with directives in order to be recognized. Choice (B) is incorrect because ExamPrep Co. would be considered a de jure corporation, not a de facto corporation. Choice (C) is incorrect because, in order to be recognized, Utopia (like most other jurisdictions) requires that a corporation file Articles of Incorporation and otherwise comply with statutory requirements. Choice (D) is incorrect because placing the ad in the newspaper was a directive, not a requirement for recognition.

2. **(C)** Choice (C) is correct because the doctrine of estoppel dictates that, if a person believed that he was dealing with a corporation (and because John saw ExamPrep Co.'s ads, he did), then neither side can deny the existence of the corporate entity. Choice (A) is therefore incorrect. Choice (B) is incorrect both because, (1) using the assumptions in this question, ExamPrep Co. is not a de facto corporation (it has never made a good faith effort to comply with the statutory requirements) and (2) a de facto corporation would have to honor its contract with John. Choice (D), while not incorrect, is not as complete an answer as (C).

3. **(B)** Choice (B) is correct because Leashes, Inc. cannot pierce the corporate veil if there has been no fraud or injustice. Choice (A) is wrong, as, under piercing doctrine, if there had been fraud or injustice, Leashes, Inc. could get a judgment against Darlene as well as against Dogwalkers, regardless of Darlene's financial status. Choices (C) and (D) are incorrect because the mere facts that Darlene is the sole shareholder or that the board of directors did not meet regularly are not enough, in and of themselves, to constitute fraud and injustice.

4. **(A)** Choice (A) is correct because, in order for Walking Doggies to pierce the corporate veil, Darlene must have committed fraud or injustice. Forming a corporation to evade contractual obligations (such as a noncompete) is an example of such fraud and/or injustice. Choice (B) is incorrect because the applicability and enforceability of noncompetition agreements are usually limited to a specific geographic area. Choice (C) is incorrect because Darlene's intent is the key factor in a court's decision in this case. Choice (D) is incorrect because an injunction could prevent Darlene from walking dogs in the future and because Darlene's financial status is irrelevant.

5. **(D)** The minority rule on pre-incorporation stock subscription agreements is that, after a corporation has been formed, all potential shareholders must agree to release each other. If they do not, the corporation may sue as a third-party beneficiary. The other shareholders did not agree to release Mohammed. Choice (A) is wrong for this reason. Choice (B) is wrong because (1) Blackacre has adopted the minority rule and (2) under the majority rule, Mohammed could only revoke his subscription before the corporation was formed. Choice (C) is wrong because it is entirely irrelevant.

CORPORATIONS

6. **(B)** Excellent Adventures only had $300 in the bank. It would cost the corporation $40,000 to lead the tour. This kind of undercapitalization is an example of fraud or injustice and would be grounds for piercing the corporate veil to reach Bill and Ted. For this reason, Choice (C) is incorrect. Choice (A) is incorrect because the question asks whether Bill and Ted would be liable, not whether Excellent Adventures would be liable. Choice (D) is irrelevant and is therefore incorrect.

7. **(B)** Although management of a corporation's affairs is vested in its board of directors, there are situations that require shareholder approval, including the sale of substantially all of the corporate assets. Choice (A) is incorrect because shareholders have approval rights in certain situations whether or not the corporation is closely held. Choices (C) and (D) are incorrect because the board of directors does not have unlimited control.

8. **(C)** Boards of directors may make reasonable charitable donations as long as an argument for long-term benefit to the corporation is plausible. Choices (A) and (B) are therefore incorrect. Choice (D), while correct, is not as strong an answer as Choice (C).

9. **(B)** Even if the board of directors acts in a manner that conflicts with the by-laws, such action may be valid as an implied amendment if the board has the power to amend the by-laws or pass a resolution in conflict with them. Choice (C) is therefore incorrect. Choice (A), while true, does not address the issue in the question. Choice (D) is incorrect because the ultra vires doctrine is inapplicable in this situation.

10. **(B)** Modernly, corporations may not raise as a defense the fact that the board's action was beyond the scope of its authority. Choice (A) is incorrect because BMC's agreement to make a charitable contribution will probably be considered to be a gratuitous promise, and not a contract. Choice (C) is incorrect because this answer refers to *common law* ultra vires doctrine, which stated that if performance had not begun, the ultra vires doctrine could be raised as a complete defense. Choice (D) is incorrect, as no one is suing to enjoin the agreement here.

11. **(D)** If an interim vacancy occurs on a board of directors, the position is usually filled by a majority of the board of directors until the shareholders may elect a new director at the next annual meeting. Choices (A), (B), and (C) are therefore incorrect.

12. **(A)** If Michael votes 451 shares for Tinkerbelle and 451 for another candidate, he will still only have 148 left, and Wendy can vote 450 for Peter. Therefore, Choice (D) is incorrect. Choice (B) is incorrect because "principles of corporate fairness" is a made-up term. Corporations try to be fair, certainly, but nothing says that they have to be! Choice (C) is incorrect because Wendy can vote for more than one director—she can split her votes however she likes; however, her best chance of getting Peter elected is to devote all of her shares to voting for him.

ANSWERS TO MULTIPLE-CHOICE QUESTIONS

13. **(D)** Under straight voting, Michael can vote (or decline to vote) all of his shares for each of the candidates for directorship. Therefore, his votes will always defeat Wendy's votes, and Peter will be defeated. Choice (A) is therefore wrong. Choice (B) is incorrect because "principles of corporate fairness" is a made-up term. Corporations try to be fair, certainly, but nothing says that they have to be! Choice (C) is incorrect because Wendy may cast (or decline to cast) all of her shares for each candidate—her votes simply will not be enough to defeat Michael's.

14. **(B)** A director can be removed by the shareholders for dishonesty, gross incompetence, or breach of his duty of loyalty to the corporation. Note that, in many jurisdictions, a director may be removed with or without cause by a vote of the shareholders, who may call a special shareholder's meeting to vote the director out. Choice (A) is incorrect because the shareholders, not the directors, vote on whether or not a director should be removed for cause. Choice (C) is incorrect because Maria was dishonest, and the shareholders may therefore vote to remove her even if her activity somehow benefited the corporation. Choice (D) is wrong because the shareholders may act immediately and need not wait until the next annual meeting to vote Maria out.

15. **(A)** If Maria is acting in a way that is detrimental to the corporation—and her bootlegging almost certainly is—then a court may remove her if the shareholders will not. However, such action is considered an extraordinary remedy that will only be used if no other remedy exists. Choice (D) is therefore incorrect. Choice (B) is incorrect because no suit is necessary if a majority of the shareholders vote to remove her. Choice (C) is incorrect because shareholders, not directors, remove directors for cause.

16. **(B)** The presence of a majority of the board members—or a *quorum*—is ordinarily necessary to pass a resolution. Choices (C) and (D) are therefore incorrect. Choice (A) is incorrect because Tom, even though he is president, cannot unilaterally make decisions on behalf of the corporation.

17. **(B)** When the board validates written resolutions but does not meet as a body to vote on them, it is called an *informal action*. Informal actions are generally permitted as long as the requisite number of members signs off on the resolution. Choice (D) is therefore incorrect. However, in most jurisdictions, actions by written consent of the directors must be unanimous to be valid. Thus Choice (B) is a more complete answer than Choice (C). Choice (A) is incorrect only because it is not the best answer. If the by-laws prohibit informal actions, then they will not be valid unless the board votes or acts to amend the by-laws.

18. **(B)** If a corporation's by-laws allow it, special meetings of the board may be called. If no time period for notice is stipulated, reasonable notice is required. Choice (C) is therefore incorrect. Choice (A) is incorrect because, while the resolution is important, Choice (B) is a more complete answer. Choice (D) is incorrect because other directors or officers may call a special meeting.

CORPORATIONS

19. (A) Defects in quorum, notice, or voting may be cured by postmeeting ratification. Choices (C) and (D) are therefore incorrect. Choice B is incorrect because the defect in notice was not immaterial and must be cured by postmeeting ratification.

20. (D) Tanya has a conflict of interest because she has a duty of loyalty to TTT but, as majority shareholder, would profit greatly from the deal between Best Burritos and TTT. Therefore, she *should* abstain from voting. Choice (A) is therefore wrong, although Tanya is allowed to vote if she can be objective and make decisions that benefit the corporation. Choice (B) would be a good answer if the question asked if Tanya *could* vote for Best Burritos, as doing so would be in TTT's best interests (and thus Tanya's vote for Best Burritos would be not only in Tanya's interest, but also would benefit TTT). Choice (C) is incorrect because Tanya *should* abstain from voting regardless of the way she plans to vote.

21. (D) If a vote of the board of directors results in a tie vote, then a provisional director may be appointed (if the by-laws allow it). Choices (A) and (C) are incorrect because no presumption exists in the case of a tie vote. Choice (B) is incorrect because it is both impractical and possibly ineffective. The board could recast its votes forever without resolving the issue!

22. (A) Prospective agreements among directors to vote a particular way are ordinarily void. Otherwise, the vote would not be spontaneous and impartial. Choice (C) is therefore incorrect. Choice (B) is incorrect because resolutions that pass may be ultimately revoked, or vice versa. A corporation is not forever wedded to decisions made at one board meeting. Choice (D) is incorrect because the directors, not the shareholders, make decisions about the operations of the corporation. The shareholders elect the directors to make such decisions.

23. (D) The board of directors appoints major corporate officers (like the president). Choices (A), (B), and (C) are therefore incorrect. Note that the shareholders elect the directors and empower them to make such decisions.

24. (D) In many jurisdictions, a vice-president may also bind the corporation to transactions that are clearly within the scope of its business. The purchasing of coffee is clearly within the scope of Legal Grounds' business, because Legal Grounds is a corporation that serves coffee. Choice (A) is therefore incorrect. Choice (B) is incorrect because the president, while ultimately responsible, must delegate responsibility and authority to other corporate officers. Choice (C) is incorrect because, while true, it is not the best answer.

25. (D) Corporate officers have the apparent authority to enter into transactions that are reasonably related to performing the duties for which they are responsible. The Corporate Coffee Grinder is responsible for grinding coffee. Therefore, he has the authority to buy equipment that will be used for coffee grinding. Choices (A) and (B) are therefore wrong. Choice (C) is somewhat correct. A corporate officer may not cause the corporation to commence bankruptcy proceedings. However, there

ANSWERS TO MULTIPLE-CHOICE QUESTIONS

is no evidence in this question that the purchase of the coffee grinder has caused Legal Grounds any financial hardship or that the Corporate Coffee Grinder has commenced bankruptcy proceedings on behalf of Legal Grounds.

26. **(C)** Where a particular corporate officer has previously entered into a kind of transaction without objection by the board, he is deemed to have been impliedly authorized to bind the corporation with regard to subsequent, similar undertakings until and unless the authority is rescinded by the board of directors. Because the Corporate Coffee Grinder has entered into these kinds of transactions before without objection, he now has the authority to do so. Choices (A) and (B) are therefore incorrect. Choice (D) is incorrect because the Corporate Coffee Grinder's capacity to contract is not based on whether or not he is an attorney.

27. **(B)** Where a corporation should have recognized that a third party would be likely to view the officer or agent as possessing the authority to bind the corporation to the agreement in question, it cannot avoid the transaction. Here, the Corporate Coffee Grinder is a corporate officer, and Legal Grounds should have recognized that others would view him as having the authority to enter into such contracts. This is called the doctrine of apparent authority. Choice (C) is therefore wrong. Choice (A) is incorrect because the corporation's needs are irrelevant to the issue at hand. Choice (D) is wrong because there is consideration here. In this bilateral contract, Legal Grounds has promised to pay money and Coffee Grinders, Inc. has promised to provide coffee grinders.

28. **(C)** Although directors usually may inspect their corporation's books and records, the corporation may refuse to allow a director to do so if she will be misusing the information. In these circumstances, a court may also enjoin a director from inspecting the books if she attempts to do so against the corporation's wishes. Here, Jocelyn would be using the information to compete with one of BBI's product lines. Choice (A) is therefore incorrect. Choice (B) is incorrect because Jocelyn would be competing with one of BBI's product lines, and it does not matter that it is not BBI's main product line. Choice (D) is incorrect because directors generally have the right to inspect their corporation's books and records.

29. **(A)** The corporate opportunity doctrine holds that a corporate director or officer may not exploit information or opportunities acquired or made available to her as a consequence of her corporate position, for personal gain, unless the corporation learns of the opportunity and declines to pursue it or cannot exploit the opportunity. Here, there is no evidence that the corporation has had the opportunity to market covers in Sleeplessness. Therefore, Jocelyn must refrain from doing so. Choice (D) is therefore incorrect. Choices (B) and (C) are incorrect because Jocelyn owes a duty of loyalty to BBI not to compete.

30. **(C)** Shareholders may challenge and recover an officer's salary if it is unreasonable and a waste of corporate assets. Choices (A) and (B) are therefore incorrect. Choice (D) is incorrect because the length of Henry's tenure is not relevant if the salary is unreasonable.

CORPORATIONS

31. (A) Directors are not automatically disqualified from being engaged in a business that is in competition with that of their corporation. Choice (D) is therefore incorrect. Choice (B) is incorrect because, while not required to disclose her plans, she may want to do so in the interests of full disclosure. Choice (C) is wrong because it is completely irrelevant!

32. (B) A director may not solicit key personnel to a competing business prior to resigning from the board. Choice (A) is therefore incorrect. Choices (C) and (D) are red herrings; the question asks about Felicia's rights, not Larry's.

33. (D) The Three Bears have several courses of action that they may take, including (A), (B), and/or (C).

34. (B) In order to have standing under Rule 10b-5, you must purchase or sell shares. Merely holding shares does not constitute a purchase or sale. Choice (A) is incorrect because the information was clearly material—the fact that the houses could be blown down would be a real problem for BuildAHouse. Choice (C) is incorrect because the Three Little Pigs did possess scienter; the facts state that they made a conscious decision not to release the information. Choice (D) is incorrect because, while the shareholders should have had the information, the Three Bears have no standing to challenge the failure of BuildAHouse to disclose it.

35. (D) Punitive damages are not available under Rule 10b-5.

36. (C) Horatio Holiday owns a controlling interest in the company. If he were to vote all of his shares for candidates for director positions, his candidates would win. Choices (A) and (B), as well as (D), are therefore incorrect.

37. (A) The majority rule states that the board of directors and a majority of shareholders must approve the sale of substantially all of a corporation's assets. Because Horatio is the controlling shareholder, his approval, in addition to that of the board, is required. Note that in some jurisdictions, where a corporation is in financial distress, shareholder approval is not required for a corporation to sell all of its assets. Note also that some jurisdictions require a higher proportion of shareholders approve such a sale.

38. (B) Where a sale of assets/inventory is made for the purpose of facilitating transfer of the business to other premises, no shareholder approval is generally required.

39. (B) To assert her rights, a shareholder must: (1) File a written objection to the sale prior to the shareholders' meeting to consider the action; (2) vote against the sale; (3) give prompt written notice of her desire to assert the appraisal remedy; and (4) surrender her shares to the corporation. A personal appearance at the shareholders' meeting is not required.

ANSWERS TO MULTIPLE-CHOICE QUESTIONS

40. (C) If the shareholders demand access to the list of shareholders eligible to vote and have a proper purpose for doing so, then HHC may grant or refuse this request. If HHC grants the request (as assumed by Choice (C)), then the shareholders should mail the materials themselves and pay the costs of doing so. If HHC refuses the request, then it must mail the materials with its own, but the group of shareholders mounting the challenge must pay the additional postage their mailing causes HHC to incur. Choice (A) is wrong because it says that the shareholders "must" research the names and addresses themselves. As explained here, they may ask HHC for this information. Choice (B) is wrong for this reason and because HHC is not responsible for the mailing costs. Choice (D) is wrong because, if the shareholder group looks in HHC's books for the information, HHC does not have to mail the materials (nor, of course, incur the costs of doing so).

TRUE-FALSE QUESTIONS
TOPIC LIST

1. Personal liability of corporate officers
2. Shareholder liability for corporate obligations
3. Subordination of corporate debt
4. Quorum
5. Ratification of acts of a corporate officer
6. Reasonable prudence of board members
7. Conflicts of interest
8. Recovery of excess salaries and bonuses
9. Director's enforcement of outstanding claims against the corporation
10. SEC Rule 10b-5—scienter
11. SEC Rule 10b-5—obligations of insiders to make disclosures
12. SEC Rule 10b-5—material misrepresentations
13. Applicability of SEC Rule 16(b)
14. Timing of ownership of shares under SEC Rule 16(b)
15. Notice requirements for special meetings of the shareholders
16. Quorum—timing requirements
17. Unanimity of voting
18. New issuances of shares
19. Payment of dividends
20. Payment of dividends
21. Shareholder standing to bring derivative actions
22. Unilateral settlement of derivative actions
23. Proceeds of a derivative suit
24. Indemnification of directors in the face of a derivative suit
25. Transfer of shares
26. Shareholders' rights to inspect the corporation's books and records

TRUE-FALSE QUESTIONS TOPIC LIST

27. Contracts between the corporation and a majority shareholder

28. Appointment of the board by a single shareholder

29. Shareholder approval of the sale of the corporation's assets

30. Approval of a merger

TRUE-FALSE QUESTIONS

(Circle Correct Answer)

1. T F A corporate officer may not be personally liable on contracts or other obligations entered into in the name of the corporation.

2. T F Shareholders are never liable for a corporation's obligations.

3. T F Corporation A goes into bankruptcy. Its debts to its shareholders may be subordinated to its debts to other creditors.

4. T F If there is not a quorum at a meeting of the board, then any decision made by the directors at that meeting is automatically null and void.

5. T F The board of directors may ratify the acts of a corporate officer, even after the act has occurred and even if the officer did not possess the requisite authority at the time that she acted.

6. T F If board members fail to exercise reasonable prudence with respect to corporate matters, they are not personally liable because they acted in their capacity as corporate directors.

7. T F If a director or officer has a direct financial interest in a potential corporate transaction, then the corporation may not pursue that transaction because there would be a conflict of interest.

8. T F A corporation may recover any excess salaries, bonuses, and other forms of compensation it has paid to its employees.

9. T F A director may acquire and enforce an outstanding claim against the corporation.

10. T F Under SEC Rule 10b-5, if a defendant did not intend to deceive someone in transferring securities, he is still liable.

11. T F Under SEC Rule 10b-5, an insider is under a duty to disclose any nonpublic information pertaining to the securities being traded.

12. T F Under SEC Rule 10b-5 if a defendant has made a material misrepresentation with respect to the sale or purchase of securities, there is a presumption of reliance by the plaintiff.

13. T F Section 16(b) of the Securities Exchange Act of 1934 applies to the sale or purchase of equity securities only.

14. T F A shareholder who wishes to initiate a derivative action under Section 16(b) of the Securities Exchange Act of 1934 need not have owned shares in the corporation at the time the transaction under scrutiny took place.

15. T F Notice of a special meeting of the shareholders need only indicate the date, time, and place where the meeting will be held.

16. T F For a quorum to be present at a meeting of the shareholders, the

TURE-FALSE QUESTIONS

persons holding the necessary shares or proxies must remain at the meeting until all matters to be voted upon have been resolved.

17. **T F** A corporation generally may not require that a vote be unanimous for a resolution to pass.

18. **T F** Under the modern rule, if there is a new issuance of shares, a shareholder may acquire the shares necessary to maintain her present, proportionate interest in the corporation.

19. **T F** A corporation is not required to pay dividends if doing so would cause it to become insolvent.

20. **T F** A corporation may pay dividends even if there is no surplus.

21. **T F** A shareholder may bring a derivative action even if she was not a shareholder at the time that the harm occurred.

22. **T F** A plaintiff has the authority to unilaterally settle a derivative action.

23. **T F** The shareholders split the proceeds of a derivative suit.

24. **T F** If, as a part of a settlement agreement, a director defendant is required to pay money to the corporation, the corporation may not indemnify that individual for his attorneys' fees and litigation expenses.

25. **T F** A corporation may prohibit a shareholder from selling or transferring shares to certain types of people.

26. **T F** Shareholders have the right to inspect the corporation's books and records at will.

27. **T F** A board of directors may enter into contracts with a majority shareholder.

28. **T F** In some circumstances, a single shareholder can appoint the board himself.

29. **T F** The board of directors does not always have to obtain shareholder approval for a sale of all of the corporation's assets.

30. **T F** The secretary of state, among others, must approve a merger.

ANSWERS TO TRUE-FALSE QUESTIONS

1. **False.**

    If the officer exceeds his or her authority, he or she may be personally liable. An officer may also be personally liable if he or she makes a personal guarantee (e.g., to repay a loan), commits a tort, or improperly represents him/herself as an agent of the corporation. Depending on the jurisdiction, an officer may also have statutory liability.

2. **False.**

    If the corporation disregards corporate formalities, commingles assets, is undercapitalized, or is predominately owned by an individual or another corporation, among other criteria, a court may "pierce the corporate veil" and hold the shareholders liable for the corporation's obligations.

3. **True.**

    Shareholder debts may be subordinated so that the corporation may pay other creditors. This is called the "Deep Rock doctrine" and derives from *Taylor v. Standard Gas and Electric Co.,* 306 U.S. 307 (1939). The Deep Rock doctrine is applied when there has been fraud, mismanagement (more than simple negligence), commingling of funds, or undercapitalization, among other reasons.

4. **False.**

    Defects in quorum, notice, or voting may be cured by postmeeting ratification (i.e., where a majority of directors (i) sign a writing that approves the resolution or (ii) fail to object after notice of the resolution is acquired).

5. **True.**

    Ratification may be explicit (i.e., passing a resolution that confirms the transaction) or implied (i.e., acceptance of the benefits of the agreement).

6. **False.**

    Directors who fail to exercise the same degree of care and skill with respect to corporate matters as a reasonably prudent person would exercise with respect to his own affairs are ordinarily jointly and severally liable to the corporation for losses resulting from their misconduct.

7. **False.**

    Where a director or officer has a direct financial interest in a transaction, he must fully disclose his interest to the board and refrain from voting on that matter. However, if a majority of disinterested directors approve the transaction, and if it is fair to the corporation, then the transaction may go forward.

8. **True.**

    If compensation constitutes a waste of corporate assets, the corporation may recover it.

ANSWERS TO TRUE-FALSE QUESTIONS

9. **True.**

   As long as the corporate opportunity doctrine is not violated (i.e., the director is not exploiting a corporate opportunity for personal gain), a director may acquire and enforce debts owed to the corporation. Note that the director is obliged to disclose the acquisition and refrain from any discussions pertaining to it if the obligation could be disputed by the corporation.

10. **False.**

    Under SEC Rule 10b-5, there is no strict liability. Scienter (the intent to deceive or take unfair advantage of another) is a requirement for liability. Negligent statements are not actionable.

11. **False.**

    Under Rule 10b-5, an insider is under a duty to disclose *material,* nonpublic information pertaining to the securities being traded.

12. **False.**

    Where the defendant has made a material misrepresentation, *the plaintiff must affirmatively prove reliance upon it.* Where there has been a failure to disclose material facts, reliance is presumed.

13. **True.**

    Unlike Rule 10b-5, Rule 16(b) only applies to equity securities, rather than evidence of indebtedness.

14. **True.**

    If the board of directors fails to initiate an action and there is a likelihood of substantial recovery, a shareholder may initiate an action even if she did not own shares in the corporation at the time of the transaction in question.

15. **False.**

    Notice of a special meeting must indicate the matters to be voted upon. However, notice of an *annual* meeting need only contain the date, time, and place of the meeting.

16. **False.**

    The majority view is that, once a quorum is present, it does not cease to exist because persons holding the necessary shares or proxies leave the meeting.

17. **True.**

    If unanimity were required, nothing would ever be passed! Furthermore, provisions requiring unanimity are ordinarily void because there is little flexibility to adapt to changing economic circumstances.

CORPORATIONS

18. False.

The rule stated is actually the common law rule. Under the common law, shareholders had that right as long as they exercised it promptly. Under the modern rule, no preemptive rights exist unless a corporation provides for them in its Articles of Incorporation.

19. True.

A corporation does not have to pay dividends (and, indeed, in most states such dividends are not allowed) if doing so would cause insolvency on the part of the corporation.

20. True.

In some states. A corporation may pay "nimble dividends"—dividends that are permissible, despite the fact that a surplus does not exist at the time distribution is made—in a few states.

21. True and False.

In order to bring a derivative action—or an action by a shareholder on behalf of the corporation—a shareholder must have owned stock at the time that the alleged harm took place. There are exceptions to this rule: a shareholder who did not own stock at the time of the alleged wrong may bring a derivative action if (1) the plaintiff acquired her shares through operation of law (i.e., inheritance), (2) the derivative action is premised upon Rule 16(b), or (3) a substantial injustice will occur unless the action is permitted.

22. False.

Settlement or dismissal of a derivative action must ordinarily be approved by the court (after notice to the shareholders).

23. True (indirectly).

Actually, the proceeds of a derivative suit (minus the attorneys' fees and expenses) go to the corporation. Because shareholders own a piece of the corporation, they indirectly benefit.

24. False.

In most jurisdictions, the corporation may pay the defendant's expenses and fees as long as a majority of disinterested directors consider the director to have been acting in good faith.

25. True and False.

A court will usually uphold as a reasonable restriction a corporation's prohibition on sales to particular types of persons, such as competitors. However, a corporation may not place a prohibition on sales of shares to specific ethnic or racial groups.

ANSWERS TO TRUE-FALSE QUESTIONS

26. True.

At common law, the shareholder had to prove that his purpose was proper (i.e., advancing the corporation's purposes in some way). However, most states now require corporations to prove that a shareholder's purpose is improper.

27. False.

If the terms are unusually favorable. This would usually be considered a breach of fiduciary duty.

28. True.

If the shareholder holds a controlling interest in the company. Such a shareholder could elect the entire board on his own, and he may therefore arrange for the seriatim resignation of current directors and appoint directors on his own.

29. True.

Under the following circumstances, the board does not need the approval of the shareholders: (1) If the sale occurs in the ordinary course of business, (2) if inventory is sold at one location for the purpose of facilitating transfer of the business to other premises, (3) if the corporation was organized for the purpose of transacting the sale (or sales) in question, or (4) in some jurisdictions, if the corporation is in financial distress.

30. True.

To effectuate a merger, the plan of merger must be approved by the board of directors of both corporations, by a majority (or, in many jurisdictions, a higher proportion) of the shareholders, and the secretary of state.

ESSAY QUESTIONS

Essay questions 1–2 refer to the following fact pattern.

Since 1991, Art has been president of Exco, a publicly held corporation with net assets of approximately $50 million. Exco manufactures computers. In 1995, Art negotiated an agreement for the purchase by Exco of all outstanding shares of Yang Inc. ("Yang"), a privately held maker of computer components, for $5 million cash. The purchase was made in early 1996. At the time, other members of Art's immediate family were holders of the outstanding shares of Yang. This information was not known except to Art, Yang's management, and Bob, an Exco director.

Art negotiated Exco's purchase of Yang stock and executed the purchase agreement on behalf of Exco, relying on his authority as its president. Before the purchase documents were signed, however, Art discussed the proposed acquisition individually with Bob, Curt, and Don. Curt and Don are Exco directors who, with Art and Bob, comprise a majority of Exco's seven-person board of directors. Bob, Curt, and Don each individually told Art that he approved the transaction.

After the purchase of Yang stock by Exco, at the next regular meeting of Exco's board in June 1996, Art informed all directors of the acquisition. While some questions were asked, there was no vote on the acquisition at the meeting. Except for Bob and Art, no other Exco director was informed of the previous ownership of Yang stock by Art's family members. Because Bob believed the acquisition was beneficial to Exco, he has never mentioned to any other Exco director his knowledge of the prior ownership of Yang stock by members of Art's family. The existence of such prior ownership could, however, have been discovered by a review of Yang's corporate records.

Since the purchase of its stock by Exco, Yang has been consistently and increasingly unprofitable. At the annual Exco shareholders' meeting in November 1997, Art, Bob, Curt, and Don were not re-elected as directors. In December 1997, the new Exco board replaced Art as president.

1. **Can Exco rescind the 1996 purchase of Yang stock? Discuss.**

2. **Can Exco recover damages for Yang's unprofitability from any or all of the following:**
   a. **Art? Discuss.**
   b. **Bob? Discuss.**
   c. **Curt and Don? Discuss.**

Essay questions 3–6 refer to the following fact pattern.

Acquirer, Inc. (Aco) and Target, Inc. (Tco) are corporations. All sales and purchases described below were conducted through a national stock exchange.

On December 1, 1996, Aco bought 120,000 Tco shares for $5 per share, thereby becoming a 12 percent Tco shareholder. Aco never previously owned any Tco stock. Aco immediately notified Tco's chief executive officer, Dan, that it had made the purchase and that it was considering a tender offer for the rest of Tco's stock at $9 per share.

The next day, Dan's personal lawyer, Len, warned Dan not to buy Tco stock until Aco's stock purchase and acquisition plans became public. On the same day, Dan told his son, Sam, about the proposed acquisition. On December 3, 1996, Len and Sam each bought 10,000 Tco shares for $5 per share.

On December 4, 1996, Aco filed appropriate disclosure documents with the Securities and Exchange Commission (SEC), and Aco and Tco separately issued press releases about the stock purchase and the proposed acquisition.

On December 5, 1996, Len and Sam each sold their 10,000 Tco shares for $8.50 per share. Aco sold its Tco shares for $9 per share on February 15, 1997.

Dan has neither sold nor purchased any Tco stock since he learned of the acquisition plan.

3. **What, if any, are the liabilities of Aco under Section 16(b) of the Securities Exchange Act of 1934? Discuss.**

4. **What, if any, are the liabilities of Dan under SEC Rule 10b-5? Discuss.**

5. **What, if any, are the liabilities of Sam under SEC Rule 10b-5? Discuss.**

6. **What, if any, are the liabilities of Len under SEC Rule 10b-5? Discuss.**

Essay questions 7–9 refer to the following fact pattern.

Starco, stockbrokers, in attempting to market 1,000,000 common shares to be issued by Durmac, offered 500,000 shares to the Ennis Corp. ("Ennis") at $50 per share. Already the owner of a substantial interest in Durmac, Ennis's financial condition was such as to make desirable a large immediate acquisition of additional shares of Durmac.

Ennis's by-laws provided that a quorum consisted of five out of its seven directors. After due notice to the four resident directors, but without notice to the three nonresident directors, a special emergency board of directors' meeting was held. Resident directors Almon, Bames, and Chester, with a proxy executed by Grabe, the fourth resident director, attended the meeting. Also present was Webster, a nonresident director. The directors present unanimously voted to purchase 400,000 of the new Durmac shares. Upon conclusion of the meeting, Webster signed a waiver of notice.

Immediately following the meeting, Ennis purchased and paid for in full 400,000 Durmac shares.

At their next regular meeting, attended by all directors, the board voted unanimously to ratify the action taken at the special emergency meeting.

Before the actual offering of Durmac shares to Ennis, Starco had offered to a select few, for one day only, a few thousand of the new common Durmac shares at $42 per share, cash. Among the offerees was Almon, who purchased a total of 2,000 shares for his own account. Almon subsequently disposed of these shares at a substantial profit. However, by the time the Ennis shareholders became aware of the foregoing facts, the market price of Durmac shares had declined sharply.

7. **Was the acquisition of Durmac shares by Ennis a proper corporate action? Discuss.**

8. **Are any of the directors liable to Ennis for the decline in value of Durmac shares? Discuss.**

9. **What, if any, is the liability of Almon to Ennis for profits he made on his purchase and sale of the Durmac shares? Discuss.**

Do not discuss federal statutory securities issues.

CORPORATIONS

Essay questions 10–12 refer to the following fact pattern.

Corp., Inc. (Corp), has 200,000 authorized shares of $1 par value stock. Andy, Ben, Carl, and Dave each purchased at par and continue to hold 50,000 shares of Corp. Corp's articles prohibit incurring any single debt in excess of $75,000 and require a vote representing 80 percent of outstanding shares to amend the articles. The articles also provide for preemptive rights, cumulative voting, and a board of four directors. Each of the four shareholders has elected himself director at annual shareholder meetings during each year of corporate existence.

Corp's board unanimously decided to borrow $100,000 from Lender. Lender took Corp's ten-year note, bearing interest at 20 percent per annum, payable in monthly interest installments. Corp has the option to pay off the note at any time, without penalty. Later, Lender needed funds and approached Andy, who serves as Corp's treasurer. Lender offered to sell the note for $90,000 and Andy, without consulting with Ben, Carl, or Dave, purchased the note on his own account.

The week following the purchase of the note by Andy, Rich asked to subscribe to 100,000 shares of Corp stock at $1 per share. Ben, Carl, and Dave approved Rich's proposal, but at the annual shareholders' meeting, Andy voted against and thus defeated a proposed amendment of the articles authorizing additional shares free from preemptive rights. Because of the note's high interest, Andy did not want it paid off. The other directors, hoping to use Rich's investment to pay the note and now aware of Andy's acquisition of it, were angered and caused Corp to cease paying the monthly interest installments.

Rich then caused the incorporation of Endrun, Inc., and subscribed to 100,000 of its shares for $100,000. Rich proposes that Corp be merged into Endrun, that each Corp share be converted into an Endrun share, and that Endrun pay the Lender note now held by Andy. Corp's board has approved the merger three to one, Andy dissenting.

Assume that the interest rate is not usurious.

10. **Did Andy breach any duty to Corp or to fellow shareholders in voting against the proposal to issue 100,000 shares to Rich? Discuss.**

11. **Can Andy obtain an injunction to prevent the Corp/Endrun merger? Discuss.**

12. **Can Andy collect interest payments on Corp's note? Discuss.**

Essay questions 13–14 refer to the following fact pattern.

Abby, chief executive officer of Oilco, was eating lunch with several fellow Oilco executives when she saw her business school classmate, Barb, sit down at the next table. Abby was aware that Barb was a prominent local stockbroker. In an unusually loud voice, Abby stated to her fellow executives, "I bet my former classmate would give her left arm to know that tomorrow we are going to announce a tender offer for ALT Corporation."

Barb overheard this remark, and, when she returned to her office, she bought 10,000 shares of ALT Corporation for her own account.

Barb also telephoned the Mutual Fund Complex (Mutual) and told its chief executive officer, "if you are smart, you will buy ALT Corporation this afternoon." Within one hour Mutual placed an order to buy 50,000 shares of ALT, using Barb as a broker.

That afternoon, Barb visited Cora, a neighbor whom she intensely disliked and who, at Barb's recommendation, had recently purchased ALT stocks. Barb told Cora that she had heard that ALT shares were about to decrease in value, and because she felt badly that it was upon her advice that Cora had purchased ALT shares, she was willing to buy the ALT shares from Cora at the current stock exchange price without charging any commission. Cora immediately sold Barb her 100 shares of ALT stock.

The following morning, Oilco announced it was making a tender offer for ALT Corporation shares at a price 50 percent above its current market price. Approximately one month later, the tender offer was completed, with Barb and Mutual receiving profits of approximately 50 percent on their shares. Abby has not purchased any ALT shares for more than three years.

13. **Has Abby, Barb, or Mutual violated SEC Rule 10b-5? Discuss.**

14. **Has Barb incurred any potential nonstatutory civil liability? Discuss.**

Essay questions 15–18 refer to the following fact pattern.

Buff is president, board chairman, and the controlling shareholder of Movie Classics Co. ("MCC"), a publicly traded corporation whose only assets are the motion picture rights to a number of famous black-and-white films produced in the 1930s and 1940s. A recent wave of nostalgia for older movies has generated greatly increased business interest in the controlling rights to films such as those owned by MCC. As a result, in the last three years, the net asset value of MCC has increased from $1.50 per share of its one class of common stock, to potentially $15 per share if MCC's film rights are appraised at their highest possible current market value. During the same period, the market price for MCC's shares has increased only one-half as much, and they presently trade at about $8 per share.

Home Videos (HV) is engaged in marketing TV DVDs of motion pictures. HV has recently offered to purchase all the assets of MCC at a premium price, which would equal $15 for each share outstanding. HV has publicly announced plans to colorize all the black-and-white films owned by MCC if the acquisition takes place. Buff has voted against accepting the HV offer because he opposes the colorization of the black-and-white films.

Buff is nevertheless very interested in disposing of his stock ownership in MCC. He would therefore like to accept an offer made by Dan, acting for an anonymous buyer, of $15 per share for all of Buff's controlling shares in MCC. This price would give Buff about the same amount of money he would obtain if HV's offer is accepted. Dan has also offered Buff an additional $2 per share for Buff's stock, if Buff and the other directors of MCC, all of whom were nominated by Buff, resign in favor of replacement directors to be nominated by Dan's principal, the unidentified buyer.

15. **What liabilities, if any, does Buff face if he accepts the offer from Dan for $15 per share of his MCC stock? Discuss.**

16. **What liabilities, if any, does Buff face if he accepts the additional offer from Dan of a premium of $2 per share for his MCC stock, for assuring the resignation of all present MCC directors? Discuss.**

17. **What liabilities, if any, does Buff face if, instead of selling his MCC stock to Dan, he sells it to HV after causing MCC to reject the HV offer? Discuss.**

18. **On what bases, if any, could a minority shareholder of MCC assert a claim against Buff, directly or derivatively, if he causes MCC to reject the HV offer? Discuss.**

Do not consider federal or state securities law issues.

CORPORATIONS

Essay question 19 refers to the following fact pattern.

Space Corporation (Space), an aerospace manufacturer, had 100,000 shares of authorized common stock, of which 85,000 shares were issued and outstanding and 15,000 shares were unissued. In need of immediate cash, Space validly issued and sold the remaining 15,000 shares to Banco Corporation (Banco) at $14 per share. The next day Adams, treasurer of Banco, was duly elected to fill a vacancy on the Space board of directors. At the first Space board meeting after his election as a director, Adams learned of a recent Space confidential study made for the board that showed that if Space did not receive governmental financial assistance, it would become insolvent. Adams immediately informed the Banco directors of the confidential study.

One month later, Senator Jones, a United States senator and a good friend of Conn, Space's main lobbyist, told Conn that in two weeks, the president of the United States would probably announce his support of the proposed Aerospace Act, then pending in the Senate. This act would provide government guaranteed loans to aerospace industry firms. Conn told no one of Jones's prediction. However, that same day, Conn purchased 2,000 shares of Space stock over the New York Stock Exchange at $15. The next day, through an agent who did not disclose that Conn was his principal, he purchased Banco's 15,000 shares of Space stock at the market value of $15 per share. In light of the confidential study, Banco was eager to unload its Space stock.

Two weeks after Jones's conversation with Conn, to the surprise of the general public, the president announced his support of the Act. Space stock immediately climbed to $25 per share.

19. Discuss the rights of Space and Banco.

Essay question 20 refers to the following fact pattern.

In 1978, Paul bought 10,000 shares of the common stock of Deco Corporation. In 1990, Deco purchased four retail stores from Savco for $4 million, which was a fair price. Tom, president and a director of Deco, was also a director of Savco. He was absent from the meeting of the Deco board of directors where the agreement for Deco's purchase of the Savco stores was considered. In Tom's absence, the proposed purchase was unanimously approved by the remaining four Deco directors, who constituted a quorum of the board.

In early 1991, the Deco directors resolved to offer 25,000 shares of authorized but unissued Deco common stock to Smith, in exchange for Greenacre, a store site owned by Smith. The directors did not offer any of the 25,000 shares for acquisition by Deco shareholders before consummating the deal with Smith.

At a meeting of the Deco board on March 15, 1992, Tom advised the board that an audit had established that Deco had incurred a $25 million loss during the preceding fiscal year, which would be publicly announced at the annual Deco shareholders' meeting on April 1st. Tom then tendered his resignation both as president and a director of Deco, effective immediately, which the board accepted.

Beginning on March 19 and continuing through March 27, 1992, Tom sold his 20,000 shares of Deco common stock for an average price of $25 per share. After the annual shareholders, meeting on April 1, 1992, the market price of Deco common stock dropped to $10 per share.

In May, 1992, Paul died. His daughter, Emma, inherited all his shares of Deco stock. Emma made three demands upon the Deco board of directors, stating that if each of the demands was not met, she, as a shareholder, would bring appropriate legal action. The demands are:

a. That the purchase of the four stores from Savco be set aside;

b. That she be permitted to purchase a number of Deco shares in the same proportion as Paul's 10,000 shares bore to all Deco shares issued and outstanding at the time of the share transfer to Smith;

c. That Deco bring suit against Tom to recover $300,000 based upon the sale of his Deco stock.

20. How should the Deco directors respond to each of the demands by Emma? Discuss.

Essay questions 21–22 refer to the following fact pattern.

Paul owns 250 of the 1,000 issued and authorized shares of Durco, a State X close corporation. The Durco directors are Al, who owns 650 shares, and Baker and Carr, each of whom owns 50 shares of Durco stock. Al has offered to buy the shares of Durco stock owned by Paul at a price substantially less than that paid by Paul to acquire the stock. Paul has refused Al's offer, claiming the offered price was "unfair."

Paul has brought an action in State X court against Durco and its three directors. His complaint alleges:

(A) The directors have acted unreasonably in failing to have Durco distribute as cash dividends approximately $5 million of accumulated earnings;

(B) The distribution is being arbitrarily withheld for the benefit of Al;

(C) There is an "invalid" agreement between the individual defendants as Durco shareholders, the purpose of which is to maintain Al in office as "managing director" to supervise and direct the operations and management of all of Durco's business;

(D) Paul has been consistently denied the right to inspect Durco's corporate records during regular working hours or at any other time.

By way of relief, the complaint asks that: (1) Al be removed as a director for misconduct; (2) the shareholders' agreement be found invalid; (3) the directors declare and pay a substantial cash dividend; and (4) Paul be permitted to inspect Durco's records during normal business hours.

In their answer, the defendants allege that Paul's action should be considered a derivative action, and admit the existence and terms of the shareholders' agreement, the withholding of accumulated earnings of approximately $5 million, and the denial of access by Paul to Durco's records. They then allege by way of affirmative defense that: (1) the discretion of the directors to declare dividends has been properly exercised; (2) the shareholders' agreement is valid and therefore Al cannot be removed as director, even for cause; and (3) the requested inspection should be denied because Paul only wants to inspect the corporate records for the "improper purpose" of bringing a "strike suit."

The defendants have moved for an order requiring Paul to post security for costs in the pending action.

State X law grants an unqualified right to shareholders of State X corporations to inspect corporate books and records, and requires plaintiffs in shareholder derivative actions to provide security for costs.

21. How should the court rule on the defendants' motion for security for costs? Discuss.

22. How should the court rule on each of Paul's requests for relief? Discuss.

Essay questions 23–24 refer to the following fact pattern.

The by-laws of Dixie, a publicly held corporation, provide, "The number of directors of the corporation shall be five." Insofar as pertinent, Dixie's Articles of Incorporation state that the number "constituting the initial board of directors" is five and provide for annual election of directors.

Since its incorporation five years ago, Dixie has been very profitable. Anticipating a hostile takeover attempt, the board voted to increase its size to nine and to stagger the terms of directors so that only three would stand for election each year.

Stan, owner of 29 percent of Dixie's voting stock, demanded that the board call a special meeting of shareholders to disapprove the board's action and to remove the president from office. The board refused to call a meeting for those purposes. It filled the newly created board positions with persons who were experienced in business and were close friends of the original board members. The new board entered into transactions that harmed Dixie financially, but which made the corporation a less attractive target for takeover.

When Stan filed a derivative suit against Dixie and the directors challenged the board's conduct, the board appointed the new members as a "special litigation committee." Thereafter, the board moved to dismiss the suit because "based upon the recommendation of the special litigation committee, the board has concluded the suit is not in the best interests of Dixie."

23. Did the board act lawfully:
    a. In increasing its size to nine members without a shareholder vote? Discuss.
    b. In staggering the terms of board members without a shareholder vote? Discuss.
    c. In refusing to call a special meeting of shareholders? Discuss.
    d. In filling the newly created board positions without a shareholder vote? Discuss.

24. Should the court grant the board's motion to dismiss? Discuss.

Do not discuss federal securities law issues.

Essay questions 25–26 refer to the following fact pattern.

Four years ago, Ida bought 50,000 shares of Martco. Three years ago, Martco contracted with Buildco for the construction of four new stores for $4 million. At the Martco board meeting at which the Buildco contract was to be considered, Chare, Martco's chairman, revealed that he had been a director of Buildco for eight years, but that he had not participated as a member of the Buildco board in approving this contract. Chare, believing it to be a fair contract, joined the other four Martco directors in voting to approve the contract. In fact, subsequent investigation revealed that the price charged by Buildco under the contract was excessive and unfair to Martco.

Two years ago, Ida died, leaving her stock to her son Sol. Unhappy about Chare's leadership, Sol asked Chare for Martco's shareholder list to solicit proxies to unseat Chare at the annual stockholders' meeting, to be held in one month. Chare, fearing Sol's success, refused, and Sol was unable to gain a seat on the board. Later Sol learned that Waters, another shareholder, would have given Sol his proxy. Between the two, they owned sufficient shares to elect one director under Martco's cumulative voting rule.

At the annual stockholder's meeting last month, Chare announced that Martco had suffered a $10 million loss during the last fiscal year and that this information would be published within 15 days in Martco's annual report. He then tendered his resignation, which was accepted effective immediately.

Five days later, Chare sold 100,000 shares of Martco stock, his entire holdings, for $25 per share, the current market price. After the loss announcement ten days later, Martco stock dropped to $10 per share. Sol asked the remaining directors to bring suit against Chare, but they refused.

Assume *no* federal securities laws are applicable.

25. **What, if any, is Chare's personal liability to Sol? Discuss.**

26. **Assuming Sol brings a shareholder's derivative action against Chare, what is the probable success of such suit in connection with the foregoing facts? Discuss.**

Essay questions 27–28 refer to the following fact pattern.

The Merryvale District of Kidstown is an affluent area where many young families live. Although there are dozens of children within a one-mile radius, there are no city-run playgrounds there. A group of Merryvale parents therefore have decided to establish a playground operation for the children who live in the neighborhood. The parents plan to find a vacant lot, raise money through the sale of memberships for construction and land purchase, and build a playground. The playground will have swings, monkey bars, slides, jungle gyms, and other typical play equipment. The parents also plan to hire supervisors to monitor the playground from 8:00 a.m. to dusk. The parents wish to maintain substantial control over the operation of the playground, and only residents of the area will be able to purchase the membership passes necessary to access it.

27. **Describe two organizational forms by which the playground could be established and operated.**

28. **The parents ask you to be their attorney in organizing the playground. Which organizational form would you recommend to them? Why?**

CORPORATIONS

Essay question 29 refers to the following fact pattern.

Three brothers—John, Jacob, and Jingleheimer Schmidt—together own 60 percent of Company Y, a privately held company in the state of Nirvana that manufactures widgets. Each brother owns 20 percent of the shares. The brothers recently inherited their ownership in the company from their father, who had owned the full 60 percent prior to his death. The rest of the shares are owned by many other shareholders, none of whom owns more than two percent of Company Y's shares. John, Jacob, and Jingleheimer are also the only members of the board of directors.

Prior to inheriting their shares a few months ago, the brothers had not been very involved in the company. John had been a freelance musician, Jacob had been working with the homeless, and Jingleheimer had been in high school. They wish to remain on Company Y's board, but, after much consideration, they are now fairly close to making a firm decision to add some outside directors to the board. As a final step in the decision-making process, they come to you for legal advice.

29. **Discuss ways in which adding members to the board could help or hurt Company Y as well as enhance or detract from the brothers' position in the company.**

Essay question 30 refers to the following fact pattern.

Bill Cheapskates, a software entrepreneur, has just graduated from college as an art history major. He is a computer guru, and he has designed some new software that makes accessing the Internet faster and easier. He has friends at several of the big Internet service providers (ISPs) (Mindspring, EarthLink, AOL, etc.) and they tell him that their companies would be interested in using the software.

Although he has visions of BMW Z-8s and European vacations running through his head, Bill does not know how much the ISPs would be willing to pay for his software or how much it would really be worth to them. Bill has not incurred much cost to date, but he is not sure how expensive it will be to bring his product to market himself.

30. **What might lead Bill to sell part or all of his ownership of the software and/or any corporate entity he establishes to market it? Why might he decide against doing so?**

ANSWERS TO ESSAY QUESTIONS

1. Can Exco rescind the 1986 purchase of Yang stock? Discuss.

There are three independent theories upon which Exco ("E") could attempt to rescind the transaction with Art's family ("Sellers").

Breach of fiduciary duty

Where a director has a personal interest in a transaction his corporation is considering, he is ordinarily obliged to (1) disclose his interest to the entire board of directors, (2) refrain from voting upon it, *and* (3) disclose any information indicating that the transaction is not in the corporation's best interests. A transaction involving a director's immediate family would probably be one in which the latter has a "personal" interest. While it is unclear from the facts as to whether Art had reason to believe that the transaction was not in E's best interests, he clearly failed to meet the initial two requirements.

Art cannot claim that the transaction was subsequently ratified by a majority of the entire board (i.e., when Bob, Curt, and Don advised him that they approved of the transaction), since (1) there was never a formal vote upon it, (2) he and Bob never disclosed to the other members of the board that Sellers were members of Art's immediate family, and (3) there was no majority explicitly in favor of the purchase if Art's vote is discounted.

Ultra Vires

The president ordinarily oversees the day-to-day operations of his corporation. While he usually has the express or inherent power to bind the corporation in routine transactions, a $5 million acquisition (constituting 10 percent of E's assets) would probably *not* be within his authority.

SEC Rule 10b-5

Under SEC Rule 10b-5, it is unlawful to employ any scheme to defraud another in connection with the purchase of a security. If it could be shown that (1) Art had reason to know that the Yang stock was overvalued, or (2) Sellers knew (or should have known) that Art was conducting the sale by himself for the purpose of paying them an excessive amount for the Yang shares, the transaction is probably illegal with respect to E.

Can E obtain rescission?

Under rescission, (1) E would tender the Yang stock to Sellers, and (2) Sellers would return the purchase price of the shares to E.

Sellers could contend that rescission (an equitable remedy, and therefore one which is discretionary with the court) is *not* appropriate, since (1) the doctrine of laches is applicable (i.e., the entire board of E was informed of the transaction one and one-half years ago, and yet no action had been taken), and (2) the decreased profitability of Yang might have been due to actions undertaken by E. Unless E can show that (1) the decline in value of Yang stock would have occurred regardless of who was managing Yang (i.e., the decreased profitability was due to unalterable market conditions), or (2) Sellers knew that Art was deliberately paying them an excessive purchase price, rescission would probably *not* be granted.

2a. Can E recover damages for Yang's unprofitability from Art?

In addition to the theories described above, a derivative action against Art might also be sustained alleging a violation of the *duty of care* (i.e., a director must exercise the same degree of care and diligence with respect to corporate matters as he would with respect to his own financial affairs). It is unclear from the facts as to whether Art investigated the transaction with the thoroughness that a $5 million acquisition deserves. Assuming (1) he did not, and (2) the price paid by E was unfair, E could probably recover from Art the diminishment in the value of Yang stock between the time of purchase and trial. This amount would be reduced to the extent, if any, that Art could show that Yang's decreased profitability was due to E's management of the operation.

2b. Can E recover damages for Yang's unprofitability from Bob?

The discussions above with respect to the duty of care and (for the most part) a director's fiduciary duties would be applicable to Bob. Although Bob did not conduct the transaction, he was probably under a fiduciary obligation to disclose Art's conflict of interest to the entire board of E (even though Bob, in good faith, believed the transaction to be beneficial to E). No action would lie under SEC Rule 10b-5 against Bob, since the scienter (desire or intent to deceive the corporation) element is lacking.

2c. Can E recover damages for Yang's unprofitability from Curt and Don?

The discussion above with respect to the duty of care would be equally applicable, since the transaction had *not* been consummated at the time Curt and Don were originally informed of the prospective acquisition.

3. What, if any, are Aco's ("A's") liabilities under Section 16(b) of the Securities Exchange Act of 1934?

Under Section 16(b), profits on matched purchases and sales (or sales and purchases) within a six-month period by owners of 10 percent of the beneficial interest of a corporation whose stock is traded on a national exchange are recoverable by that corporation. However, the stockholder must have *already* held 10 percent or more of the shares at both the time of the purchase and sale. Since A's purchase of Tco ("T") stock merely enabled it to become a 10 percent shareholder, Section 16b would be applicable here only to the sale of T stock by A after it became a 10 percent shareholder of T. With no matching purchase after A became a 10 percent shareholder, A has no liability under Section 16(b).

ANSWERS TO ESSAY QUESTIONS

4. What, if any, are Dan's ("D's") liabilities under SEC Rule 10b-5?

Under 10b-5, one who misuses nonpublic ("inside") information of a material nature (i.e., which would cause a reasonable person to purchase or sell the stock in question) to acquire stock which subsequently appreciates in value is liable to (1) those persons who may have sold the stock in question, and (2) in certain circumstances, the SEC. Tippers also have potential liability under this provision.

To determine if D has liability under 10b-5, it is necessary to ascertain how he transmitted information of A's impending tender offer. SEC Rule 10b-5 is not operative unless an instrumentality of interstate commerce (i.e., the telephone, mails, etc.) was used in some manner. If D's comments to Sam and Len were made in face-to-face encounters (i.e., over a lunch or dinner table), D would have no liability under 10b-5.

Assuming, however, D's conversations with Sam ("S") and Len ("L") occurred over the telephone, D could claim that the scienter (i.e., the intent or knowledge that the inside information would be used by the party to whom it was communicated) element is lacking. With respect to L (D's personal lawyer), D would probably have assumed that the latter would not use the information in an illegal manner. With respect to S, more facts are needed to assess the likelihood that D should have realized S would use the information of A's tender offer (i.e., had S displayed an interest in the stock market prior to D's comments, did he have sufficient spendable income to invest in stocks, etc.?).

Finally, D might also argue that the information was not material, since A indicated only that it was "considering" a tender offer. However, the facts that (1) both L and S acted promptly upon receipt of D's comment, and (2) T's stock almost doubled in price immediately after the tender offer became public, tend to show that the "material" element was satisfied.

Assuming D lost on the foregoing issues, what is his potential liability? If it is impossible to determine the actual sellers of the T stock that S purchased (i.e., the purchases were made over a national stock exchange), each of the persons who sold T stock over the exchange on December 3 (but prior to the time of S's purchase) could probably recover $3.50 per share (the difference between the value of T stock once news of the tender offer was fully known and the sales price). If none of the potentially aggrieved sellers commenced an action, the SEC could (1) compel S to disgorge his profit to it, and (2) recover from D an amount equal to S's profit from the information.

5. What, if any, are S's liabilities under SEC Rule 10b-5?

Assuming S (1) did, or should have, realized that he had been made privy to inside information, and (2) in some manner, used an instrumentality of interstate commerce in connection with his purchase of T stock, the discussion above with respect to D's potential liability would also be applicable to S.

6. What, if any, are L's liabilities under SEC Rule 10b-5?

Assuming L used an instrumentality of interstate commerce in connection with his purchase of T stock, there would appear to be little doubt that he is liable to the persons

CORPORATIONS

who sold T stock over the exchange on December 3 (but prior to the moment of L's purchase). Again, in the event that none of these persons commenced an action against L, the SEC could oblige him to disgorge his profit.

Finally, it might be mentioned that punitive damages have not been permitted under a 10b-5 civil action.

7. Was the acquisition of Durmac ("D") shares by Ennis ("E") a proper corporate action? Discuss.

First, even if the two directors who were not present had voted against the purchase of D shares, it would not have affected the decision to purchase the stock. Second, if it could be shown that it was not physically possible for the absent directors to be present at the meeting (even had notification occurred), a contention that the meeting was invalidly held would be further undermined. Finally, if it could be shown that the other two nonresident directors had somehow heard of the meeting (as Webster did), the notice requirement might be deemed to be satisfied despite the lack of compliance with any formal requisites set forth in the by-laws or Articles of Incorporation. Thus, the failure to formally notify the three nonresident directors would probably *not* constitute a valid basis for attacking the decision to purchase D stock.

In most jurisdictions, an interested director must disclose any possible conflict with respect to a matter that is being voted upon by the board. Additionally, he is ordinarily required to refrain from voting on such a matter. Thus, it could be contended that Almon's ("A's") attendance at the meeting should have been discounted, which arguably would have resulted in the lack of a quorum. However, the inability of an interested director to vote on a matter does not ordinarily require him to be discounted for purposes of a quorum. Finally, even if A had refrained from voting upon the acquisition of D's stock, there would still have been four directors voting in favor of the decision (presuming that a simple majority is all that is necessary for action by the board to be taken). Therefore, the acquisition of D's shares by E was probably a proper corporate action.

8. Are any of the directors liable to Ennis for the decline in value of Durmac shares? Discuss.

A corporate director is required to exercise the same due care with respect to corporate matters as he would with respect to his own financial affairs. The facts are silent as to whether A or the other members of E's board should have realized that the market price of D shares could decline sharply. It is also unclear as to whether A had a special reason to perceive the decline in D stock in view of his earlier opportunity to purchase it at $42 per share. If A was aware of the possibility of an imminent decline in D's shares, he would have had a fiduciary obligation to disclose such information to E's board of directors. If he failed to do so, and if it was likely that such data would have dissuaded the board from deciding to make the acquisition, A would be liable to the shareholders of E in a derivative action for the losses resulting from the decline of D stock.

ANSWERS TO ESSAY QUESTIONS

Assuming the decline in D's stock was the result of unanticipated market conditions that could not have been perceived with a diligent investigation by E's board, the latter group would probably have no liability to its shareholders. On the other hand, since E was expending $2,500,000, it is possible that the board of directors violated the duty of care by hurriedly making such a substantial acquisition. Such a major expenditure should arguably have been undertaken only after a careful investigation of D had been made.

Assuming E's board was deemed to have violated the duty of care, the two nonresident directors could probably not successfully defend against liability, since they later ratified the action taken at the emergency meeting. Additionally, Grabe would probably also be liable under the theory that he assumed the risk of an inappropriate vote when he gave Chester a proxy.

9. What, if any, is the liability of Almon to Ennis for profits he made on his purchase and sale of the Durmac shares? Discuss.

E could attempt to recover from A under the corporate opportunity and "special facts" doctrines.

Under the former theory, a director is obligated to refrain from gaining any personal advantage to the detriment of his company as a consequence of information derived from his corporate position. Thus, E's board could contend that A should have (1) advised it of the possibility of purchasing D stock at $42 per share, and (2) permitted E to purchase the shares at that rate. However, the facts are silent as to whether (1) the offer to A was made as a consequence of the latter's position at E, and (2) whether A had reason to believe that D stock would subsequently be offered to E at a higher rate. Assuming either inquiry was answered in the negative, A would not have liability to E under the corporate opportunity doctrine.

Under the "special facts" doctrine, where a corporate insider with knowledge of extraordinary information unknown to the public sells stock to an existing shareholder, he may be liable for the failure to disclose such information to the extent of the profit made or loss avoided. Modernly, some courts have extended the right to sue to the insider's corporation, if the defrauded shareholders fail to bring an action. First, the special facts doctrine only permits the corporation whose shares were traded to recover the profit made from the corporate insider. In this instance, A is not being pursued by D (but rather by E). Also, the facts are silent as to whether (1) A had reason to believe that D's stock was going to decline sharply at the time he sold his shares, (2) he had any inside information as to the imminent decline of D's stock, and (3) the purchasers of the shares were already stockholders of D. If any of these inquiries were answered in the negative, there would be an additional reason why the special facts doctrine could not be successfully applied to A. In summary, it is unlikely that A has any liability to E.

10. Did Andy breach any duty to Corp or to fellow shareholders in voting against the proposal to issue 100,000 shares to Rich? Discuss.

It is well established that majority shareholders cannot exercise control in a manner that is injurious to the minority. Conversely, a minority shareholder should not be permitted to act in a manner that promotes his interests to the detriment of the other members of the corporation. Ben, Carl, and Dave (the "Other Shareholders") could argue that by causing Corp to continue to pay an unusually high interest rate pursuant to the note, Andy has wrongfully exercised a "veto power" over Corp's attempt to preserve its assets.

Andy could contend in rebuttal, however, that he was not obliged to relinquish his pre-emptive rights, especially since as a consequence of Rich obtaining 100,000 shares he would (under cumulative voting) lose the certainty of sitting on Corp's board of directors. The facts are silent as to whether (a) Rich would have been willing to buy only 75,000 shares, (b) the Other Shareholders would have been willing to permit Andy to purchase 25,000 additional shares, and (c) Andy had the financial ability and desire to purchase an additional 25,000 shares (thereby retaining his 25 percent interest in Corp). Assuming it could be proven that all of these conditions would have been satisfied, Andy probably did not breach his duty of loyalty to Corp. Under these circumstances, Andy should have been given the opportunity to maintain his equity position in Corp unless the interest paid on the note was significantly affecting Corp's profitability and operations in a detrimental manner.

11. Can Andy obtain an injunction to prevent the Corp/Endrun merger? Discuss.

Mergers ordinarily require approval by the board of directors and a specified proportion of shareholders. Some jurisdictions require that only a majority of shareholders approve a merger, while other states impose a higher proportion (ordinarily two-thirds). If the merger can be accomplished in accordance with Corp's presently existing articles and by-laws, Andy would contend that the majority shareholders are breaching their fiduciary duty to him by diluting his 25 percent ownership interest. However, assuming the Other Shareholders can show that their motivation was to preserve Corp's assets by terminating an excessive financial obligation, they would probably prevail.

If a merger is deemed to be an "amendment" of Corp's articles (thereby requiring Andy's authorization), the resolution of this issue would depend upon a consideration of the unknown factors discussed above with respect to whether Andy breached a fiduciary duty to Corp.

Were Andy to prevail on the substantive issues, there would appear to be no difficulty in a court issuing an order which restrained both Corp and Endrun from consummating the merger.

12. Can Andy collect interest payments on Corp's note? Discuss.

Directors owe a fiduciary duty of loyalty to their corporations. As a consequence, they are obligated to refrain from gaining any personal advantage to the detriment of their corporations. The Other Shareholders could contend that, pursuant to this duty, Andy was obliged to have advised them of the ability to acquire Lender's note for 90 percent of its face value (thereby saving $10,000 of principal and subsequent interest payments). Assuming Lender approached Andy with the thought of permitting Corp (as opposed to Andy, individually) to purchase the note, Andy would seem to be firmly within corporate opportunity doctrine. Even if Lender approached Andy in his individual capacity (i.e., as his friend, rather than as Corp's treasurer), most jurisdictions would probably still conclude that Andy was obliged to disclose Lender's offer to the other directors before taking advantage of it himself.

Assuming Andy breached his duty of loyalty by not communicating Lender's offer to the other members of Corp's board of directors, the Other Shareholders would probably be obliged to show that they could have raised the $90,000 demanded by Lender (i.e., obtained a loan, authorized and purchased additional stock, etc.). If Corp could have purchased the note, Corp can probably now acquire it from Andy for $90,000, less whatever interest was paid by Corp subsequent to the time Andy obtained ownership of the note. If Corp could not have acquired the note when offered to Andy by Lender, Corp would probably be liable to Andy for the accrued interest.

Corp might also contend that the note is unenforceable under the ultra vires doctrine (Corp's articles prohibit incurring any single debt in excess of $75,000, and the principal amount of the note was $100,000). However, since the entire board of directors (which was coincidentally all of the shareholders) approved the loan, the resolution would probably be looked upon as some type of informal amendment to the articles. Thus, it is unlikely that an ultra vires defense by Corp would be successful.

13. Has Abby, Barb, or Mutual violated SEC Rule 10b-5? Discuss.

ANSWER A

A. **Rule**

Under Rule 10b-5, it is a violation of the Securities Exchange Act of 1934 to use the mails, an instrumentality of interstate commerce, or a national stock exchange to make a misrepresentation of material fact, to make an omission of material fact, or to disclose material information under a duty not to, with regard to the purchase and sale of securities. Irrelevant for purposes of Rule 10b-5.

B. **Abby's Liability**

Because Abby did not purchase or sell shares of ALT by omitting a material fact or making a misrepresentation, she can only be held liable as a tipper of material information.

1. **Tipper Liability**

   A tipper of material nonpublic information is liable under Rule 10b-5 if the tipper is a fiduciary of the corporation with a duty not to disclose, he discloses material information in violation of this duty, and he tips the information recklessly or for some personal benefit.

   Here, Abby is the CEO of Oilco, who was about to make a tender offer to ALT. As CEO, Abby had a fiduciary duty to Oilco not to release that information. The information is also material, as it would induce people to purchase ALT stock prior to the announcement of the offer, which would probably cause the price of ALT stock to rise.

Additionally, while it is unclear whether Abby revealed the information for personal benefit, perhaps to gain a better relationship with Barb, her release of the information was reckless in that she stated in a loud voice, in a restaurant, that the tender offer would take place. These words were also directly aimed at Barb, "my former classmate," which does also indicate some personal benefit purpose.

Because Barb then used this information to purchase ALT stock for her account, Abby would be liable under Rule 10b-5 as a tipper.

C. **Barb's Liability**

1. **Tippee Liability**

   A tippee of material nonpublic information may also be liable under Rule 10b-5 if the tipper received the information from an insider with a fiduciary duty not to disclose, the tippee knew that the fiduciary was breaching a duty by disclosing the information, and the fiduciary was tipping for personal benefit or recklessly.

   Here, as mentioned above, Barb received the information from Abby, Oilco's CEO, who had a fiduciary duty to Oilco.

   Barb also knew, or should have known, that Abby was breaching her duty. Being a stockbroker, Barb would know that a tender offer announcement is confidential information. Furthermore, because Barb was Abby's classmate, she knew that Abby was CEO and had a fiduciary duty not to disclose.

   Finally, as mentioned above, Abby's acts were either reckless or done for the purpose of gaining some personal benefit by having Barb learn of the information.

   Therefore, by using the information to purchase ALT stock, Barb is liable under Rule 10b-5 and must return her profit to ALT.

2. **Liability as Tipper**

   Barb should not be held liable as a tipper for giving the information to Mutual as Barb was not under a fiduciary duty to keep the information private. She was not connected in any way to Oilco or ALT. Furthermore, Barb did not tell Mutual what the information was.

3. **Misrepresentation to Cora**

   Barb may be liable to Cora under Rule 10b-5, as she made a misrepresentation of material information to Cora regarding the sale of securities.

ANSWERS TO ESSAY QUESTIONS

However, because no mails, exchange, or mode of interstate commerce was used, as a face-to-face transaction occurred, Rule 10b-5 would not be applicable. This is true even though under Rule 10b-5 one does not have to be an insider to be liable when making a misrepresentation. However, all of the other above requirements must be met.

D. **Liability of Mutual**

Mutual would not be liable as a tippee of nonpublic material information.

Mutual received the tip from Barb, who was not an insider. In addition, Mutual did not receive any of the information. All that Barb said was, "If you are smart, you will buy. . . ." Mutual was entitled to rely on this statement, as Barb was a stockbroker, and her statement was objectively viewed as advice from a stockbroker.

Additionally, Mutual had no way of knowing that Barb received the information from an insider.

Therefore, although Mutual purchased ALT securities on the basis of Barb's tip, which came as a result of her learning about material nonpublic information, Mutual is not liable.

ANSWER B

1. **Abby's liability**

   Purchase or sale of stock

   First, there must be a transaction involving the purchase or sale of stock in interstate commerce. While Abby did not, in fact, buy or sell any stock of ALT in the last three years, the stock of ALT is presumably traded over a national exchange because Barb, a broker, was able to execute trades in the stock. In addition, because Abby will probably have liability as a tipper of material nonpublic information in the sales and purchases by Barb, Cora, and Mutual, there is a purchase or sale of stock that is sufficiently related to Abby's statements that were heard by Barb to satisfy this element.

   Misrepresentation or omission of material fact

   Second, there must be a misrepresentation or omission of material fact. A material fact is one that a reasonable investor would consider in making a decision as to whether to buy or sell the stock. Certainly, the fact of ALT being bought by Oilco is such a material fact, because it would clearly affect the decision to purchase or sell ALT stock, as most tender offers are at a price higher than the then-current market price of the stock. The issue is whether there has been a misrepresentation or omission. There is clearly no misrepresentation, as the facts stated by Abby were true. However, the courts have taken the position that giving out material inside information to some people but not others by a person with a duty to disclose is an omission. Therefore, Abby's telling her fellow executives of the tender offer loudly enough so that she knew Barb would hear it was giving inside information, and was an omission of material fact so long as Abby had a duty to disclose the information. As the CEO of Oilco, Abby is an officer and therefore an insider of Oilco. As such an insider, Abby has a duty to disclose any inside information to the public generally if she discloses it to anyone. Therefore, her disclosure of the information to Barb, without disclosing it to the public generally, was a material omission.

A Proper Defendant

Third, Abby must be a proper defendant. This means that she must be someone who has bought or sold stock in connection with the inside information, or be a tipper. A tipper is someone who is an insider who gives inside information to another, and who benefits from having given that information. Here, Abby is clearly an insider and has given inside information to Barb. She has benefited from this information presumably, or she would not have given it. The benefit does not need to be monetary and, here, the benefit presumably is that she had the opportunity to show off to Barb as to her knowledge about pending transactions and her importance. Therefore, Abby is a proper defendant.

A Proper Plaintiff

Next, there needs to be a proper plaintiff. This is anyone who bought or sold the stock. This would include Cora, any others who sold their stock at the time that Barb or Mutual was buying, the SEC, and the corporation.

Reliance

Next, these plaintiffs had to have relied on any misrepresentations that were made. However, since this is a case involving an omission rather than a misrepresentation, no reliance is necessary.

Damages

Finally, the plaintiffs have to have suffered injury. Here, clearly Cora and the people who sold their stock to Barb and Mutual have suffered injury as, if they had not sold their stock because of Barb and Mutual's use of inside information, they would have made 50 percent on their stock the next day.

Insider Status

An interesting issue is whether Abby should really be considered an insider since she was an insider of Oilco and the stock that was being sold on insider information was the stock of ALT. While a close call, Abby should probably be considered an insider of ALT as a constructive insider, because she was someone in a position of confidence with ALT because she knew this information regarding the proposed tender offer. In addition, the courts have found people who know about the future acquisitions of stock by tender offers to be insiders for Rule 10b-5 purposes.

ANSWERS TO ESSAY QUESTIONS

Scienter

The final element that must be proven is scienter, or intent on the part of Abby. Here, it is clear that she had the appropriate scienter since she clearly intended that Barb be given inside information and she spoke loud enough to insure that Barb, in fact, heard the information.

2. **Barb's Liability**

   Barb could be liable under Rule 10b-5 for three separate transactions. These are: buying stock on her own account as a tippee, buying stock from Cora, and tipping Mutual to buy stock.

   Tippee Liability

   Turning first to the tippee liability, Barb will be liable under the same elements as Abby if she was found to be a tippee. Here, the other elements are clearly present. She bought stock on an exchange, making it a purchase of stock using the instrumentalities of interstate commerce. She did not disclose material facts before making the purchase, there were defendants who were proper, she had scienter, as she intended to trade on inside information, and there was damage to the persons from whom she bought the stock.

   The issue here is whether she was a tippee so that she had a duty to disclose the inside information before purchasing ALT stock such that her failure to disclose was a material omission. To be a tippee, one must get inside information from an insider or a constructive insider, one must know that the information is inside information, one must act on the information, and the person who provided the information must have benefited from that act. Here, as discussed above with respect to Abby, Abby is an insider, and Abby benefited from the passing of the information to Barb. In addition, Barb knew the information was inside information based on the way that Abby told it to her and based on the fact that she was able to get away with lying about it to Cora. Therefore, Barb is liable under Rule 10b-5 for buying the stock on her own account as a tippee.

   Purchase from Cora

   Here, the elements of Rule 10b-5 are even more clearly present.

   First, there was a purchase and sale of stock, from Cora to Barb. The issue is whether it involved interstate commerce. Here, it is unclear whether Barb used any instrumentalities of interstate commerce to buy the stock, as she did not use an exchange and visited Cora in person, presumably in the same state. Interstate commerce is easy to find, however, and if Barb called Cora to tell her she was coming over, or arranged for the stock she bought from Cora to be transferred to her name on the corporate records of ALT through the mail or the phones, interstate commerce will be found.

   Second, there was a material misrepresentation here. Barb misrepresented the facts about ALT's future value. However, an argument can be made that this was merely a statement of opinion, not of fact. Due to the way it was presented to Cora, however, it should be viewed as a fact. It was certainly material because it went to the value of ALT's stock.

Third, there was reliance by Cora on the misrepresentation by Barb, as she sold her stock to Barb based on it.

Fourth, there was scienter, because Barb intended Cora to rely on the misrepresentation and sell the stock, which she did.

Fifth, Cora is a proper plaintiff because selling the stock to Barb damaged her.

Finally, Barb is a proper defendant because she was the one who made the misrepresentation to Cora.

Tipper Liability

Barb's tipper liability is based on the same elements as Abby's, with two exceptions. First, there is a closer question as to whether Barb is an insider of ALT, because she has no confidential or deemed confidential relationship with ALT. It may be, however, that her relationship with Abby is enough. In addition, her benefit from tipping Mutual of the stock transaction is that she made commission for buying ALT stock for Mutual. Therefore, Barb is probably liable under 10b-5 for tipping to Mutual.

3. **Mutual's Liability**

Mutual could be liable under 10b-5 as a tippee for having purchased ALT stock on inside information from Barb. Here, there is a purchase of stock by Mutual in interstate commerce because it was bought through a broker.

In addition, there will be an omission found, and Mutual will be a proper defendant if Mutual has tippee liability. Here, Mutual probably does not have tippee liability, because there is no indication that it knew that Barb's recommendation to buy ALT stock was based on inside information.

14. Has Barb incurred any potential nonstatutory civil liability? Discuss.

ANSWER A

A. **Misrepresentation or Deceit**

Barb may be liable to Cora under a tort theory for intentional misrepresentation.

1. **Prima Facie Case**

    The prima facie case for intentional misrepresentation involves a misrepresentation of material fact, scienter (knowledge of the misrepresentation), intent to induce current performance, reliance, justifiable reliance, and damages.

ANSWERS TO ESSAY QUESTIONS

a. **Misrepresentation**

Barb, by telling Cora that the ALT shares were about to decrease in value, made a misrepresentation of material fact, as the shares were really going to increase. The statement was material because it was important to a decision to sell the stock.

b. **Scienter**

Barb knew that the statement was false, because she had already heard from Abby about the tender offer, and any good stockbroker knows that a tender offer will make the stock of the offeree company go up.

c. **Intent to Induce Reliance or Action**

Here, the facts indicate that Barb purchased the stock from Cora after making misrepresentations. Because Barb knew the stocks were going up in value, it can be inferred that she intended to have Cora sell her the stock so that she could make a big profit.

d. **Reliance**

Cora, by selling Barb the shares, did so in reliance on Barb's misrepresentation, because it is unlikely that Cora would have sold without Barb's statement, and, had she known the truth, she certainly would not have sold.

e. **Justifiable Reliance**

Cora's reliance was justified because she knew that Barb was a stockbroker and was experienced in stock matters. Additionally, Cora bought the stock upon the advice of Barb. Therefore, Barb's statement that "she felt badly" supplies justification for Cora to rely on her statements as Barb's explanation for wanting to purchase the shares is very plausible.

f. **Damages**

By selling the shares to Barb, Cora suffered damages, because the next day the tender offer was announced, and the stock was being bought at 50 percent higher than its market value.

B. **Remedies**

Barb should be liable to Cora for the amount of profit that Cora lost as a result of the misrepresentation. In the alternative, Cora should be allowed to have a constructive trust imposed on the shares that Barb got from Cora, if Cora still holds them. A constructive trust is an equitable remedy to prevent unjust enrichment of a party who obtains property wrongfully.

CORPORATIONS

ANSWER B

A. **Barb's Common Law Liability**

Under the common law, all corporate insiders have a duty to existing shareholders who purchase or sell stock. Here, Barb bought stock from Cora, an existing shareholder. Therefore, if Barb was an insider, she had one of three duties to Cora, depending upon the jurisdiction.

In one type of jurisdiction, Barb had no duty to Cora and would have no liability.

In another type of jurisdiction, Barb would be obligated to disclose any special facts before buying stock from an existing shareholder. Here, the fact that Barb knew that ALT was to be a tender offer prospect was a special fact, so Barb had a duty to disclose that to Cora.

In the last type of jurisdiction, Barb had a duty to disclose any material facts she knew. Again, the facts here would be material facts, so Barb had a duty to disclose them to Cora before buying.

The issue is whether Barb is an insider for these purposes. Under the common law, insiders were only officers, directors, controlling shareholders, and majority shareholders. Since Barb was none of these, she had no duty unless she could be found to be a constructive insider under the analysis described above.

If Barb were an insider of ALT, she would also be liable, under the Diamond doctrine, to ALT for all of her profits on all of her stock transactions as there is a duty from insiders to corporations not to trade on inside information.

In addition to common law insider trading, Barb may also be liable to Cora for intentional misrepresentation. This tort requires that Barb intentionally misrepresent a material fact. See above for the analysis of these factors with respect to Barb's statements to Cora. In addition, the statements had to be false, as these were, and there had to be justifiable reliance on the facts, which Cora had since she was reasonable in relying on the statements made about a stock by a prominent local stockbroker. Cora actually relied because she sold the stock, and she was injured by losing the profit she would have made if she had held the stock one more day.

15. **What liabilities, if any, does Buff face if he accepts the offer from Dan for $15 per share of his MCC stock? Discuss.**

Breach of fiduciary duty (as an MCC director).

A corporate director ordinarily stands in a fiduciary duty to the entity's shareholders.

If acceptance of HV's offer was clearly in the interest of MCC's other shareholders (i.e., it would be unlikely that the value of these shares would, in the foreseeable future, exceed $15 each), Buff ("B") arguably breached his fiduciary duty of good faith by failing to recommend acceptance of HV's offer to the MCC shareholders (assuming approval by the latter group was necessary for such a sale).

However, if B held a majority of MCC shares, and could have personally vetoed the sale of MCC assets to HV, B would probably have no liability under this theory. Under these circumstances, recommendation of the sale by the board of directors to MCC shareholders would have been a futile act.

Breach of duty (as shareholder)

While a shareholder may ordinarily sell his shares to anyone he wishes, a few jurisdictions have ruled that the seller of a controlling interest must share any "premium" received from a buyer who is likely to undertake actions which will devalue the shares held by the remaining shareholders.

Since B is only aware of an "unidentified" buyer (and therefore has no reason to believe that his sale of MCC shares will result in detriment to the other shareholders), his sale to Dan at $15 per share would not appear to expose him to liability.

16. **What liabilities, if any, does Buff face if he accepts the additional offer from Dan of a premium of $2 per share for his stock, for assuring the resignation of all present MCC directors? Discuss.**

Pursuant to the valid sale of a controlling portion of stock, the buyer can ordinarily require the seller to request the resignations of the directors that the latter caused to be elected. Otherwise, the new controlling shareholder would have to await the next shareholders' meeting to elect corporate management. Thus, B probably has no liability for receipt of a premium in exchange for obtaining the resignations of MCC's present board of directors.

17. **What liabilities, if any, would Buff face if, instead of selling his MCC stock to Dan, he sells it to HV after causing MCC to reject the HV offer? Discuss.**

As discussed above (section 1), if the sale of MCC's assets is in the best interests of its shareholders, B would have breached his fiduciary duties by failing to recommend acceptance of HV's offer to the other directors and (if necessary) shareholders.

If shareholder approval was unnecessary, B is liable to MCC's other shareholders for their losses (probably the difference between $15 and the present value per share, $8). Under these circumstances, B would have, in effect, appropriated a *corporate opportunity* by causing rejection of HV's offer to the corporation and then taking personal advantage of it.

18. **On what bases, if any, could a minority shareholder of MCC assert a claim against Buff, directly or derivatively, if he causes MCC to reject the HV offer? Discuss.**

CORPORATIONS

As discussed above (section 1), if B wrongly caused MCC to reject the HV offer, he would probably be directly liable to the other MCC shareholders for breach of his fiduciary duties. The latter could recover the difference between the HV offer price and the value of their MCC stock at the time of trial.

19. Discuss the rights of Space and Banco.

Space ("S") v. Conn ("C")

Special Facts

Under the "special facts" doctrine, where a director, officer, or key employee, possessing knowledge of special facts (i.e., unusual or extraordinary information) about his corporation by reason of the position he occupies at that entity, buys its stock from an existing shareholder without disclosing such facts, the latter person can either rescind the transaction or obtain the difference between the stock's market price when the special facts become known and the price actually paid.

C would contend that this doctrine is *not* applicable because: (1) he learned of the act as a consequence of being Jones's friend, rather than as a result of his corporate position, (2) Jones merely made a prediction (rather than stating a fact) to C, and (3) S didn't suffer any direct injury from C's actions.

S could argue in rebuttal, however, that (1) Jones advised C of the imminent legislation in the latter's capacity of S's lobbyist, so that C could marshal his resources to assure passage of the act, (2) Jones's statement was in the nature of a fact (as shown by the act's passage into law shortly thereafter), and (3) some jurisdictions permit a corporation to recover under the "special facts" doctrine where the aggrieved buyer fails to do so.

The foregoing issues will probably be resolved in favor of S. Thus, S should be able to recover C's profit from the purchase of S's stock.

S would not appear to have a cause of action against C under Section 16(b) of the Exchange Act, since he was not a 10 percent shareholder when S's stock was acquired. Also, Rule 10b-5 is not applicable because this rule gives no right to a corporation to recover for insider trading in which it was not involved.

S v. Adams/Banco (16b)

Duty of Loyalty

S probably has no right of action against Adams ("A") or Banco ("B") for breach of the duty of loyalty, since S appears to have suffered no losses from Adams's disclosure.

ANSWERS TO ESSAY QUESTIONS

Section 16(b)

Under Section 16(b) of the Exchange Act, however, profits, made by an owner of more than 10 percent of the shares of stock of a corporation listed on a national securities exchange, resulting from the purchase and sale of the stock of that corporation within a six-month period, may be recovered by the corporation or its shareholders (through a derivative suit). Since B, via its deputization of Adams, was a director when the shares were sold, S could probably recover B's $1 per share profit under Section 16(b).

B v. C

Rule 10b-5

Under Rule 10b-5, the failure by a buyer to disclose nonpublic, material facts, in connection with the purchase of stock via an instrumentality of interstate commerce, gives rise to an action for rescission or damages (the difference between the sales price and the market price following disclosure of the material information) by the seller against the buyer.

C would contend that (1) again, a material "fact" is not involved, (2) if the facts as developed so indicate, no instrumentality of interstate commerce was utilized (although, if a telephone was utilized in arranging the transactions, this would probably suffice), and (3) the doctrine of pari delicto is applicable against B, because B (based on the secret report) believed that S stock would decrease in value. B should prevail on the last issue, since to hold C liable would promote the federal policy of discouraging insider trading.

Special Facts

B would also probably sue C under the special facts doctrine. The issues discussed above with respect to S's lawsuit against C would be equally applicable (except for the portion pertaining to a corporation's right to recover from an insider). The pari delicto defense would also be raised in this litigation. Based upon the conclusions reached above, B should prevail.

B v. J

Rule 10b-5

Under Rule 10b-5, tippers are liable to a seller, where they should have known that the tippee would misuse the information in question. If B sought to recover from Jones under Rule 10b-5 for tipping C, Jones would probably contend that (1) he had no intention to assist in a scheme to defraud (the information was given to C for the legitimate purpose of assisting C with his job of facilitating legislation favorable to S), and (2) to permit a lawsuit against him would allow B to obtain a double recovery (once against C, and once against him). While B might contend that the potential of a double recovery would promote the federal purpose of discouraging fraud in the sale of securities, Jones apparently lacked the scienter to deceive others. Thus, Jones should prevail.

20. How should the Deco directors respond to each of the demands by Emma? Discuss.

The first and third acts about which Emma ("E") is complaining were primarily done to Deco ("D"), rather than to herself, personally. Thus, in determining how the directors must respond, it must initially be determined if she could successfully assert a derivative action.

The directors might contend that since E was not a shareholder at the time of the alleged wrongs (she did not inherit the stock until 1992), she cannot bring a derivative action. However, in most jurisdictions, where the plaintiff has inherited the stock from someone who was a shareholder at the time of the alleged wrong (as Paul was), they may prosecute a derivative action. Additionally, in some states, a majority of the disinterested shareholders must concur in the bringing of the derivative action (if the purported wrongs could be ratified by the shareholders). However, we'll assume no such rule exists in this jurisdiction, and so no demand is necessary. Thus, a derivative action by E is possible.

Could the directors set aside the purchases of the four stores from Savco?

Since Tom was also a director of Savco ("S") at the time of the purchase, he probably was "interested" with respect to D's purchase of the S stores. Transactions involving interested directors can usually be set aside, unless (1) there is a disinterested quorum, (2) the interested party discloses his interest, (3) it is approved by a disinterested majority, and (4) the transaction is fair. The only point that could possibly be put in issue is Tom's failure to disclose his interest in S (assuming it was not known by the other directors). However, since the transaction was fair, nothing would have been gained from such a disclosure by Tom. Additionally, two years have passed since the transaction, and so it is impractical to attempt to unwind it now. Thus, the directors should respond negatively to E's first demand.

Will E be permitted to assert her preemptive rights with respect to the 25,000 shares issued to Smith?

A shareholder often has the right to buy newly issued shares in a proportion equal to her existing stock ownership. However, this right does not extend to previously authorized (even though not theretofore sold) shares. Additionally, preemptive rights often do not apply to situations where stock is exchanged for assets needed by the corporation. Thus, this demand should be rejected by the directors.

Can the directors recover the $300,000 saved by Tom?

There are three possible theories that the directors could assert against Tom to recover the $300,000 loss avoided by him.

ANSWERS TO ESSAY QUESTIONS

Rule 10b-5

Under Rule 10b-5, a corporate insider who fails to disclose a material fact with respect to the purchase or sale of stock may be liable to the buyer for the difference between the sales price and the value of the stock after the nondisclosed information became known. However, since D did not sell the shares, there would be no lawsuit by D in this instance, and so the directors should reject E's demand upon this ground.

Section 16(b)

Under Section 16(b) of the Exchange Act, the profit made or loss avoided by a sale or purchase, or purchase and sale, of stock by a corporate director, officer, or 10 percent shareholder, within any six-month period, can be recovered by the corporation. The corporation must be listed on a national security exchange or have (1) assets of no less than $3,000,000, and (2) at least 500 shareholders. Assuming the latter requisite is satisfied, D has no cause of action under Section 16(b) because the facts indicate only that T sold D stock (rather than purchased and sold). The fact that Tom had resigned prior to his sales of D stock would not be relevant, since he presumably purchased the D stock while a director of D. Thus, the directors should refuse E's demand to commence a lawsuit against Tom on this ground.

Special facts doctrine

Under the common law special facts doctrine, where a corporate insider fails to disclose special facts (i.e., those of extraordinary significance) with respect to a sale of stock to an existing shareholder, the latter can recover back from the vendor the difference between the price paid and the value of the stock when the special fact became known. A few courts have held that the corporation involved can recover the loss avoided by the insider, if the aggrieved shareholder fails to seek recovery. In this instance, however, there is no indication that Tom sold his stock to persons who already held Deco shares. Thus, the directors should refuse E's demand to sue Tom under this doctrine, too.

21. **How should the court rule on the defendants' motion for security for costs? Discuss.**

State X requires plaintiffs in a shareholder derivative suit to provide security for costs. A derivative action is one in which the harms complained about were done primarily to the corporation, rather than to the individual shareholder/plaintiff. Defendants ("D's") will contend that the refusal to distribute profits and the agreement to maintain Al as the managing director impact upon all of the shareholders, rather than upon Paul ("P") individually, and so the action is derivative nature. However, since the gist of P's action is that the other shareholders (and their appointed directors) are attempting to freeze him out of the corporation, his lawsuit is primarily personal in nature; therefore D's motion for security will probably be denied.

CORPORATIONS

22. How should the court rule on each of Paul's requests for relief? Discuss.

Al may be removed for misconduct.

A director may ordinarily be removed for good cause (fraud, gross incompetence, breach of the duty of loyalty, etc.). P could contend that Al has breached his duty of loyalty to the corporation (i.e., all of the shareholders) by putting his own personal desires (i.e., the purchase of P's stock in Durco) over his corporate duties (i.e., to pay dividends when there are funds in excess of those which are necessary for operating expenses). Since a controlling shareholder has a fiduciary duty to refrain from exercising his influence in a manner which oppresses minority shareholders, if P could prove that Al has orchestrated an effort to hold back dividends (which would otherwise be payable to P) for the purpose of inducing P to sell his Durco stock to Al, P's request for dismissal of Al should be successful. While Al (as a 65 percent shareholder) could still presumably elect the new director who would be chosen to fill his vacancy, and therefore the D's might contend that removal of Al would be ineffectual and so should not be undertaken, Al's forced departure would nevertheless impress upon the other directors the importance of their fiduciary duties toward all of the corporation's shareholders. Thus, Al should be removed.

The shareholder agreement was invalid.

While shareholder agreements (contracts whereby shareholders have agreed to vote their shares with respect to shareholder matters in a particular way) are ordinarily valid, shareholder agreements pertaining to the management of a corporation are permissible only if (1) made with respect to a close corporation, and (2) the agreement involves only a minor encroachment upon the directors' managerial discretion. Here, however, the agreement in question was to retain Al as "supervising director" (i.e., presumably, Al would instruct the other directors how to vote on matters pertaining to the management of the corporation). Thus, P's contention that it is invalid is probably well taken because permitting one director to virtually dictate all management decisions probably constitutes more than a minor encroachment upon management. Decisions would be made by a solitary person, rather than after a give-and-take discussion and majority vote of three individuals. Thus, again P should prevail.

The directors should declare and pay a substantial cash dividend.

While D's have asserted the protections of the business judgment rule (directors are not liable for corporate actions undertaken in good faith and with the same degree of care as they would exercise with respect to their own matters) with respect to the nonpayment of dividends, this argument will probably fail since their actions don't appear to have been undertaken in good faith (i.e., the objective was to "freeze out" P), and P could presumably show that the D's have reserved a much greater amount of funds than are necessary to continue the business of Durco. Thus, funds in excess of that which is necessary to operate Durco should be distributed to the shareholders.

ANSWERS TO ESSAY QUESTIONS

P should be permitted to inspect Durco's records.

The State X statute unqualifiedly authorizes shareholders to examine the books and records of their corporations. While the D's might contend that it should be implied in the plain meaning of the statute that inspection of corporate records should not be compelled where the shareholder's objective is improper (and a "strike suit" would be such an instance, because its purpose is simply to make a bad faith claim against the corporation), since P arguably desires to review the documents for a legitimate purpose (i.e., to determine how much profit should be distributed in the form of dividends), P should prevail in this instance too.

23a. **Did the board act lawfully in increasing its size to nine members without a shareholder vote? Discuss.**

Stan ("S") could contend that increasing the size of the board to nine members was illegal, in that this action contravened both the Articles of Incorporation and by-laws of Dixie. The directors of a corporation must ordinarily act in conformity with these documents. The directors might argue in rebuttal that (1) the articles don't expressly limit the number of directors to five (they state only that the "initial" board shall be comprised of five directors), and (2) corporate by-laws often permit amendment by directors (except as to actions which impact significantly upon the business operations of the corporation, such as a sale of its assets). However, S could probably successfully respond that (1) articles can ordinarily be altered by shareholder action only, and (2) enlarging the board is an action sufficiently significant to require shareholder approval (even if the directors may ordinarily amend the by-laws). Thus, increasing the number of directors was illegal.

23b. **Did the board act lawfully in staggering the terms of board members without a shareholder vote? Discuss.**

Since this action is explicitly contrary to the articles (which provide for annual elections of directors), it is probably unlawful. While the board might contend that staggered terms still permit the annual election of some directors (probably three are elected each year), the ordinary meaning that persons would attach to "annual election" is that the entire board would be elected at that time.

23c. **Did the board act lawfully in refusing to call a special meeting of shareholders? Discuss.**

Although directors, officers, and (usually) 25 percent shareholders may notice a special meeting, there is ordinarily no obligation upon the board to call such a meeting (unless the articles or by-laws require that the action sought to be accomplished must be approved by shareholders). Since S (as a 29 percent shareholder) is probably empowered to call a special meeting of shareholders, the board is not obliged to undertake this action. Additionally, only the board of directors (not shareholders) can ordinarily remove the president. Thus, the board acted correctly.

23d. Did the board act lawfully in filling the newly created board positions without a shareholder vote? Discuss.

Whether this action was proper or not depends upon what the articles or by-laws of Dixie allow. Ordinarily, the by-laws of a corporation provide that vacancies in the board may be filled by a majority of the directors. Thus, in the unlikely event that the enlargement of the board was legal, the directors probably acted lawfully in filling the vacancies.

24. Should the court grant the board's motion to dismiss?

In some states, a derivative action cannot be maintained if a majority of the directors, in good faith, determine that the lawsuit would not be in the corporation's best interests. However, where the derivative action asserts wrongdoing by a majority of the directors, director disapproval will ordinarily *not* preclude the lawsuit. The facts are silent as to whether the entity seeking a takeover had a reputation for looting corporations over which it gained control. If it did not, the board's action in enlarging the number of its members and staggering terms would appear to have been undertaken for its own self-interest (to protect director positions), and to the detriment of the corporation (presumably, the additional directors are paid by Dixie). In any event, as discussed above, the board's actions appear to be unlawful.

Additionally, while the new board members are experienced in business, their judgment seems to be questionable (the new transactions entered into by them have proven to be financially harmful). It is unclear from the given facts as to whether the recent business setbacks would result in liability of the board for breach of the duty of care.

While the board might contend that the determination to dismiss the derivative action was made by a disinterested portion of that body (the four new members), this argument should fail. The new members are close friends of the original directors and would (presumably) lose their positions if the derivative action was successful. They are therefore not "disinterested." If S's derivative action includes an allegation that the directors breached their duty of care (as opposed to simply demanding that the board's actions in increasing the number of directors and staggering their terms was unlawful), none of the directors is disinterested. Thus, the court should *not* grant the board's motion to dismiss.

25. What, if any, is Chare's personal liability to Sol? Discuss.

Where a director breaches a duty that runs primarily to the corporation, an individual shareholder must bring a derivative action. The only transaction that could yield direct liability of Chare ("C") to Sol ("S") would arise from C's refusal to give S the shareholder list.

A shareholder ordinarily has a right to inspect corporate books and records for any reasonable purpose. While C might contend that the request for the shareholder list to unseat him is not reasonable, S could probably successfully argue in rebuttal that, given Martco's past dismal performance, his demand was proper.

ANSWERS TO ESSAY QUESTIONS

S might, however, have difficulty in establishing damages. Since S and Waters could have elected only one director (S), S could claim loss of a director's compensation. However, it appears doubtful that with one seat on the board, S could have (1) avoided Martco's ("M's") losses that year, or 2) prevented C from remaining on the board.

26. Assuming Sol brings a shareholder's derivative action against Chare, what is the probable success of such suit in connection with the foregoing facts? Discuss.

S could conceivably bring a derivative action based upon (1) M's contract with Buildco, (2) the $10 million loss suffered by M during the previous fiscal year, and (3) the losses avoided by C with respect to the early sale of his stock. While a derivative suit must usually be brought by one who was a shareholder at the time of the alleged wrong, an exception to this rule normally exists for persons who acquired their shares by inheritance (as S did from Ida). In some states, a further requirement of a derivative suit is that a majority of disinterested shareholders concur in the action. However, we'll assume this condition is not operative or is waived in view of C's refusal to deliver a shareholders list to S.

M's contract with Buildco

Duty of loyalty

Directors owe their corporations a duty of loyalty to refrain from acting with respect to matters in which they have a conflict of interest. While S would argue that C is liable for M's losses since he voted for the Buildco transaction, C could argue in rebuttal that (i) he disclosed the conflict, (ii) the contract would have been approved whether he voted for it or not, and (iii) he acted in good faith (actually believing the contract was fair). C should prevail (especially since the transaction is about four years old and everyone acted honestly).

Duty of care

C (and the entire M board of directors) might, however, be liable to S, if it can be shown that they failed to exercise reasonable care in not thoroughly investigating whether the Buildco agreement (a $4 million transaction) was excessive prior to signing it. If C (and the other directors) are liable under this theory, the corporation's damages would be the difference between the actual contract price and what a fair price would have been.

M's losses during the previous fiscal year

The discussion in the preceding paragraph pertaining to reasonable care would be applicable to the $10 million loss suffered by Martco during the previous fiscal year. If it could be demonstrated that these losses occurred by reason of the director's negligence (rather than market conditions), C (and the other directors) would be liable to the extent such losses could have been avoided by the exercise of reasonable business judgment.

CORPORATIONS

C's sale of M stock without disclosure

In some states, a corporate insider with knowledge of "special facts" (i.e., extraordinary information not known to the public) must disclose them to a purchaser who is also a stockholder in that corporation. C's knowledge of M's $10 million loss would be important to a prospective purchaser (as shown by the sharp drop in the stock's price after the information became public).

C would argue that (1) the information was known to the public, since the losses were disclosed at an annual shareholder's meeting, and (2) usually only purchasers of the stock can sue for losses caused by the nondisclosure. However, in *Diamond v. Oreamuno*, directors selling their shares without disclosing inside information were held to have breached a duty *to the corporation*. If (1) this view was followed in this jurisdiction, and (2) the number of shareholders at the annual meeting was relatively small, C is probably liable to M for the losses that he avoided by his sale of M stock prior to publication of the annual report.

27. **Describe two organizational forms by which the playground could be established and operated.**

Limited Liability

The parents should consider an entity that has limited liability. This would eliminate the use of a general partnership but would shield the parents from personal liability.

Subchapter "S" corporation

A subchapter "S" corporation would be a good choice because any losses would flow through to the owners of the entity to the extent of capital contributions and undistributed accumulated earnings. The entity would still insulate them from personal liability. An "S" corporation is taxed as a partnership. The shareholders are taxed and also receive profits and losses. An "S" corporation may not have more than 75 shareholders, however, which might or might not be a problem in this case, depending on how many parents want to be a part of the playground venture. The shareholders are ordinarily limited to individuals who are residents of the United States, which would not be a problem here, as all of the potential shareholders are residents of Kidstown.

Limited Liability Company

An LLC is a noncorporate business entity whose members (the owners) can participate actively in its management but still retain limited liability. An LLC can exist either at will or for a term, and it can be managed by either member or nonmember managers. Distributions in an LLC are made either equally to each member or in proportion to each member's contribution, depending on the statute. LLC's do not issue shares of stock. Members may qualify by buying an ownership interest, which they can sell or transfer as they wish (in this case, perhaps if they move away or if a family's children grow too old for the playground).

ANSWERS TO ESSAY QUESTIONS

28. The parents ask you to be their attorney in organizing the playground. Which organizational form would you recommend? Why?

Advantageous characteristics of an LLC

A good choice for the parents would probably be a limited liability company (LLC). Because the playground is a small, neighborhood enterprise, it is unlikely ever to be publicly held. An LLC organizational form can be advantageous for a nonpublicly held business because it can be taxed as a partnership, there are few restrictions in the structuring of ownership interests and management, there are no limits on the number or nature of the owners, and there is limited liability for managers and owners.

Lack of personal liability

If the parents choose an LLC, any losses will flow through to the parents while insulating them from personal liability. Here, there is a lot of potential for accidents to occur. On a playground with equipment like slides and jungle gyms, children might fall or otherwise be hurt. Although the parents plan to hire supervisors, those supervisors cannot be everywhere at once and would be unlikely to be able to prevent such accidents. Parents tend to be very protective of (and thus litigious about) their children. Therefore, the parents will want to shield themselves from personal tort liability.

Managerial aspects

The parents plan to hire supervisors for the playground but remain very involved in its operation. This is another reason that an LLC would be a good choice. The members of an LLC are not required to manage the entity, but they may do so. Establishing an LLC will allow the parents to decide on their level of involvement over the life of the entity.

Tax advantages

Finally, because the parents are largely affluent (the facts state that it is an affluent neighborhood), an LLC may offer tax benefits. Distributions in an LLC flow through to the owners. If the parents believe that the entity will initially lose money (as most do), they might want to take the losses personally and report them on their personal tax returns. Since the parents are upper class, they may benefit from claiming any losses, and any profits probably will not rocket them into a higher tax bracket.

Drawbacks

It is true that an LLC can be expensive to organize and maintain because of the requirement to prepare documentation and maintain certain formalities; nevertheless, because of the nature of the business, it would be preferable to a general partnership or a limited partnership (the latter form requiring a general partner who would have unlimited liability). The LLC therefore offers the most advantages and the fewest drawbacks.

CORPORATIONS

29. Discuss ways in which adding members to the board could help or hurt Company Y as well as enhance or detract from the brothers' position in the company.

Adding members to the board would probably be beneficial to Company Y, but it would have benefits and drawbacks for the brothers.

Benefits to Company Y

Adding outsiders to the board would be beneficial to Company Y. This addition could add expertise to the board, as well as independence (the ability for disinterested parties to make an objective analysis). If the brothers find outside directors who are skilled and knowledgeable in the area of widget making, then the board will be much stronger. The facts state that John, Jacob, and Jingleheimer had not been involved in the company, and their previous positions were not in the area of widget-making or even business. Therefore, the addition of some outside directors will be an important and beneficial step for Company Y.

Benefits to the brothers

There are ways in which the addition of outside directors could be beneficial to the brothers. If there are other people helping to run the company, the brothers will not need to be quite as involved in or responsible for the decision making at Company Y. Perhaps they enjoy their current careers and would like to continue with them instead of devoting all of their time to widget making. Furthermore, if the brothers remain the only board members, they alone will be making decisions that affect Company Y's earnings. As the majority shareholders in Company Y, the brothers will care deeply about Company Y's potential to generate profits. Because they have little widget-making or business experience, they will be unlikely to be successful alone in leading Company Y to profitability.

Adding additional board members would also insulate the brothers from conflict of interest issues. Because the board is currently composed only of the three brothers, and because the three brothers are also the majority shareholders, conflicts of interest must inevitably arise. As it stands now, the brothers can act in their own interest with no checks and balances (other than the risk that the shareholders will sue them through a derivative action or directly for breach of fiduciary duty). There are no other directors to vote against them and no shareholders with sufficient votes to overrule them. The additional board members could be members of a special committee to deal with conflict of interest situations and affiliated transactions.

Adding additional directors will heighten the board's credibility and allow the brothers to meet their duty of care (i.e., make decisions in the best interests of the company). Therefore, the addition of outside directors would increase the minority shareholders' confidence in Company Y.

ANSWERS TO ESSAY QUESTIONS

Drawbacks for the brothers

While beneficial in some ways, however, the addition of outside directors would have some drawbacks for the brothers. The question does not state how many board members would be added. Outside directors might have sufficient votes to block the brothers from taking certain action they would want to take. The brothers may want to add only two outside directors so that they can retain control of the board; however, adding several more would give the board a greater depth of experience. Of course, as they are the majority shareholders, the brothers as a block can simply vote out any director they do not like, so no decision that they make as to the number of outside directors is irrevocable.

In making their decision, the brothers will need to weigh the potential loss of control against the clear benefits to Company Y and themselves.

Voting as a block

The previous parts of this answer presuppose that the brothers vote as a block and agree on all issues. Such may not be the case. If one brother is often outvoted by the other two, it will be to that brother's obvious advantage to convince his brothers to add other members to the board, as he may be able to convince the outsiders to vote with him. If the lone brother can convince at least 31 percent of the shareholders to vote with him, he could even remove his other brothers from the board. Similarly, the other two brothers may want to campaign the minority shareholders to vote the third brother out. Because of these possibilities, the three brothers only have control of the company if they consistently vote together. The potential for interfamily conflict is another reason that Company Y would benefit from the addition of outsiders to the board.

Conclusion

The addition of outside directors would be beneficial to Company Y and to the brothers. The brothers might experience some loss of control over the company, but, as they are the majority shareholders, any such loss would not be irrevocable. They stand to gain a great deal in terms of ability to run the company and in profits earned if they add additional directors. The addition of persons will also provide independence, objectivity, and greater assurances that the law will be complied with.

30. **What might lead Bill to sell part or all of his ownership of the software and/or any corporate entity he establishes to market it? Why might he decide against doing so?**

Several factors might lead Bill to sell part or all of his ownership of the software and/or any corporate entity he establishes to market it. However, should he decide to do so, several drawbacks would also exist for him.

CORPORATIONS

Raising of capital

In order to develop, manufacture, promote and market his product successfully, Bill will need to raise money. Because he has recently graduated from college, it is unlikely that Bill has much money of his own. To get a product to market costs a great deal. Therefore, Bill may want to sell a portion of his ownership in the product in exchange for seed capital to set up his company and market his product.

Immediate profit

If Bill were to sell all or part of his ownership interest now, he could realize some immediate profits. The facts state that he has not incurred much cost to date. Any money he received for part or all of his product, then, would be mostly profit to him. Bill may want to simply sell out, walk away, and lead a leisurely life. Selling all of his interest, of course, would mean that Bill would not receive any profits that his product would earn in the future if it turned out to be a hit. Furthermore, any portion of his interest he sells today will be at today's value. If his product is successful, the interest will be worth much more in the future.

Assistance with developing the product and running a company

If Bill were to sell all or part of his ownership interest, other investors would play a part in running the company. These other investors would necessarily have a say in the way the product was developed and marketed, but if Bill were to sell only a small portion of his ownership interest, he could maintain control while obtaining guidance and support from investors who would probably be more experienced in the business world than he, an art history major, would be.

Loss of control

If Bill were to sell all or part of his ownership interest, he would lose control of all or part of any entity he had set up to market this product. He would also lose control of all or part of the direction that the product's development would take. Instead of answering only to himself, he would have to answer to the other investors as well. This problem could easily be solved, however, if Bill were to sell only a small portion of his interest. He would then maintain control, even if he still had to answer to other investors.

Conclusion: a balance

The problem Bill faces, then, is how to retain enough of his ownership interest to maintain control of his product while raising enough money to get it to market and successfully sell it. This is the classic dilemma faced by entrepreneurs.